EVOLUTION
REVOLUTION

EVOLUTION
REVOLUTION

Conscious Leadership
for an Information Age

ABIGAIL **STASON**

Evolution Revolution
Conscious Leadership for an Information Age
Text Copyright © 2017 by Abigail Stason

For more information or to book an event, contact CMS Special Sales at (801) 635-4821 or chrisbizzz@comcast.net.

BookWise Publishing
12707 S. City Park Way
Riverton, Utah 84065
bookwisepublishing.com

Cover Design: Martine Cameau
Interior and Back Cover Layout and Design: Francine Platt, Eden Graphics, Inc.
Production and Editing: Karen K Christoffersen
Cover image used under license from shutterstock.com

Library of Congress Cataloging-in-Publication Data
Names: Stason, Abigail, author.
Title: Evolution Revolution / by Abigail Stason
Description: BookWise Publishing Paperback Edition. / Riverton, Utah, 2017
Summary: Join the evolution revolution.
Become the person you truly are and want to be.

Library of Congress Control Number: 2017956597

ISBN 978-1-60645-196-0 (CS Paperback $14.99)
ISBN 978-1-60645-198-4 (e Book $9.99)

1. Main Category Non-Fiction—Spirituality
2. Sub Category Non-Fiction—Leadership

First Edition

2 4 6 8 10 9 7 5 3 1

Printed in the United States of America

11/7/2017

To all of you who want to wake up—

thanks for being on this journey with me.

TABLE OF CONTENTS

PART TWO—UNCONSCIOUS BIAS AND STEREOTYPING

PART THREE—DO YOU HAVE YOUR BACK?

PART FOUR—GO DEEPER—GO DIRECT

PART FIVE—JOIN THE REVOLUTION

PART ONE

Conscious Leadership for an Information Age

CHAPTER 1

THE EVOLUTION REVOLUTION

In a world where industries are being turned upside down, a new paradigm for leadership is being revealed, affecting how we interact and co-exist in the world. There is a higher vibration, and a higher level of existence evolving.

Knowledge and the ability to collaborate are some of the most essential commodities in this information age, requiring agility, strength of mind, and maturity to meet the demands for what lies ahead. Every industry is affected by technology. In fact, technology is advancing faster than we are as a species, and we're playing catch up. It is through the workplace that we can meet this challenge. Our next revolution is *evolution*.

> *Businesses by their very nature bring people together. However, we spend very little time teaching people how to be in a relationship with each other. It is through relationships and love that we can expand into the truth and evolve both spiritually and as a human species.*

A new paradigm is emerging where being connected is the number one goal. It is through authentic human connection that business is transformed, and we consciously evolve.

Notice the consequences of unconscious behavior through global crises. The financial services meltdown, national and international healthcare issues, climate change, a divided country, a deformed justice and educational system, socioeconomic penalties, racism, addiction, and gender discrimination are some of the examples. They present to us the results of an uninvestigated life running on autopilot. We can no longer exist this way; it is not sustainable nor satisfying.

The crisis that is critical to each of us is our *journey*. As individuals, we contribute to everything, from our current condition to the conditions around us, both locally and globally. We can no longer afford to run on autopilot if we are to lead more fulfilling lives and create a sustainable world. This journey requires that we make different choices that are in alignment with who we are. It's time for conscious human evolution, and relationships are an accelerated path for growth.

Simple but Not Easy

As we awaken and face the truth of the changes that are taking place, we'll encounter challenges on multiple levels. Love, compassion, and understanding for the human condition are the top priorities. People, especially in the workplace, must know how to be truthful and *real* and exercise the ability to create a nervous system to support the evolution of humanity.

Imagine a world where we connect and collaborate efficiently and authentically. Here we can have an impact for the greater good of everyone on the planet. We can interact with our whole being and not merely our egos. This world is a place where our work is easeful, where we experience the integration of work and personal lives, and every interaction is a learning moment, evolving and moving into a connected, innovative, fulfilling existence. This is the world *being called forward.*

Conscious Leadership is a Practice

My friends, colleagues, and clients have repeatedly asked, "How do I become more conscious? How do I create a more fulfilling life? How may I be more effective? How do I remain connected to others? How may I become enlightened? How do I wake up and still live in this world? How can I accomplish this while still fulfilling my responsibilities?"

I am also often asked, "To solve for all of the above, is the goal to get rid of my ego?" My response is always, "*Absolutely not!*" The ego is a necessary function of being a human being. It provides structure for our bodies and minds to navigate the world. The goal instead is to develop an ego as a more evolved function.

Even though business brings us together, we've never been taught how to interact while taking a product to market: how to show up authentically while achieving an objective; how to fully express ourselves from the truth of who we are; or how to collaborate and get along. We aren't taught the answers to all these questions.

When we know how to navigate our experience with others through collaboration—when we are conscious—we create an unparalleled opening for human connection and discovery. It is this connection that leads to increased vitality, innovation, productivity, and evolution. It takes energy to show up fully, drop your stories, and get real. The following practices for Conscious Leadership are powerful and simple, but not always easy. Dedicated energy will shift your way of being. *Practice is necessary.*

If you are an achiever, a business leader, an entrepreneur, an influencer; if you are open-minded and want to bring compassion and love to your organization or into your life; if you want to bring your spirituality into your day-to-day activities; if you are ready to thrive, then keep reading. It is possible to be real, spiritual, and in the truth of who you are while achieving goals and making an impact.

Using Evolution Revolution

- Part One guides you through a series of skills you can implement in your daily life to wake up and be more conscious.

- Part Two introduces how to recognize your stereotypes and

biases and discuss them in a way that is not harmful. To be a conscious and evolved person, you must be aware of tendencies to exclude rather than include others.

- Part Three concentrates on building skills involving self-concept and avoiding the Imposter Syndrome.

- Part Four delves deeper into ways of ending the suffering of identification with your thoughts.

- Part Five is a challenge to wake up and start evolving.

The Evolution Revolution is more of an instruction manual than anything else. Personally, I embody everything in this book and have found that my life is much easier as a result. But don't take my word for it. Rely on your direct experience by trying it for yourself.

We'll begin with the essential skill—*presence*.

CHAPTER 2

PRESENCE—THE FOUNDATION FOR CONSCIOUS EVOLUTION

The practice of presence is the foundation for Conscious Evolution. It is the foundation for *everything* and the spark for growth and lasting change. The overarching questions are: "What am I present with right now? How am I present to myself at this moment?"

Presence is being with what *is*, precisely as it is, and directly, clearly, and fully inhabiting our experience. Directly experiencing life aligns us with reality, and reveals the truth of who we are.

This is presence.

> *We are at a pool. Perhaps we're discussing the temperature of the water, how we should jump in, whether we will like it, if it's dangerous, how much chlorine is in it— an infinite number of thoughts and discussions about what it will be like to be in the pool are possible. Presence is about doing what we are doing while we are doing it; that is, being in the pool and experiencing it directly versus <u>talking</u> about being in the pool.*

Presence is being in a state of flow, or borrowing a term many athletes use, being in the "zone." When in a state of flow, time disappears, and everything is of an easeful nature—even the most intense experiences.

To be present also means to be mindful, conscious, and not resist what's happening, willing to notice what's true in any situation and learn about anything at any time. We may drift from awareness, but we may become curious again.

Ask yourself this question: from what state of being would I rather be interacting or making business decisions? Present or not present? Do I want my authentic, true self to oversee my experience, or do I want my mind chatter running the show? Do I want to *talk* about my experience or *be* in my experience? The easy and powerful answer is *Yes*! I want *real* connection. *It all starts with me.*

Benefits of Presence—Being Present and Not Present

PRESENT	NOT PRESENT
In the pool	Talking about being in the pool
Being connected	Being right or getting my way
Constantly learning	Maintaining conflict
Emotions add wisdom	Curbing emotions
In the moment	In the past or future
Win for all	Personal or team agenda
Appreciation	Criticism
Innovation	*This* is the way
Compassion	Fear
Breath and movement	Adrenaline
Taking responsibility	Hero, Victim, Villain
Quality of action	Quantity of action
Childlike wonder	Childish perturbation
Doing from being	Doing from mind
Truth and reality	Stories and mind chatter
Conscious commitments	Unconscious patterns
High self-concept	Imposter Syndrome

When we are present, we are more loving and compassionate with ourselves and with others. No one person is perfect. As we learn to have compassion for the human condition, we experience more connection. We all have our patterns of thinking and behavior. By being present with our patterns and not resisting them, we can treat each other with respect, within healthy boundaries. This phenomenon makes for a more delightful work environment and overall existence.

The benefits of presence include efficient use of time, real connection, easeful collaboration, access to creative capacities, and increased vitality. When we are present, we are fully empowered and in charge of our experience. We can connect with others in a more profound and meaningful way and gain experience, wisdom, and insight. This wisdom, plus cognition, makes for a compelling combination.

The Characteristics of Being Present

- We are open to and see more possibilities.
- We are mindful.
- We are breathing and free of constriction.
- Everyone is our ally, not our enemy.
- We take responsibility for our part of any situation.
- We collaborate creatively.
- We easily feel and express emotions.
- We organize our activities around the truth of the moment.
- We are curious.
- We are continually learning and growing from every experience.
- We easily laugh at ourselves and with others.
- We seek connection and contribution over anything else.
- We accept others, ourselves, and all situations.
- We stretch our observed reality and use it as a starting point for action.

Through presence, the energy we might expend in conflict and tension can be redirected to connection and innovation. Productivity significantly increases when we harness our energy through presence. We are open and available to allow room for mistakes to happen and learn and grow from those experiences. Creative ideas and solutions appear. Space and capacity for experiences keep us from feeling constricted.

We drift from presence not just in the workplace, but in our entire lives—in relationships with coworkers, spouses, friends, family members, children, money, food, and even our creative capacity. We can be *alone* and drift from presence, even during meditation. Presence is a practice that applies to all facets of our being.

Recognizing How We Drift from Presence

When we deny the truth of the moment in any form, reject what is here, or resist our current experience, we have drifted from presence. Consciousness is about awareness, not perfection. Consciously recognizing when we have drifted from presence empowers us to take responsibility for our experience and respond to life with aligned ability and action. Only you know the truth of your experience and can determine if you are present or not present.

Here are two predominate ways we drift from presence:

The Drama Triangle. The ego drives our behavior, responding by putting on masks or personas to hide our authentic, genuine self and create a dynamic.

Mind Chatter. Mind chatter overtakes reality and organizes our activities around a false narrative. We create a state of being based on stories, illusions, a false narrative, and we are not dealing with the facts of any situation. Our lives *become* an illusion, and we begin to organize our activities around what is *not* real.

Example. Vanessa received an email from her manager on a Monday.

It read "Because of what you pointed out here, the project won't go as planned." Notice he never said the project wasn't going well, but she assumed the following narrative: "I'm in trouble. He didn't like my suggestions. The project is going to fail. I will lose my job."

Vanessa went home that night and spoke with her husband. He intuited this from when she said, "I'd better work on my résumé." He agreed and began to worry since *she* was the primary breadwinner, and he felt the pressure of needing to provide more than he currently was.

The next day, she told two of her colleagues. One of them offered to introduce her to a headhunter. That evening, she said to her husband that she was going to start looking for another job.

Wednesday, she spent the day in internal drama, worrying about her career, as well as trying to connect with a headhunter. She spent the day proofreading her résumé. Her colleagues also spent the day in drama, worried that their friend would be leaving their team and the project.

At midday Thursday, Vanessa received a follow-up email from her manager: "I want to follow-up on my last note. As I said, because of what you pointed out, the project won't go as planned. I had time to consider your ideas, and you've brought to light some issues that, when resolved, will improve the project. I reviewed your points with others and would like to meet with you today so we can regroup." Her narrative was very far from the truth of the situation.

In my review with her, she realized how much time she'd wasted that week lost in a false narrative she had created in her mind. Her actions aligned with it. She avoided her manager. She lost sleep and was exhausted. She spent very little quality time with her kids. She and her colleagues were unproductive. Her husband experienced stress. This client is a high performer, a high achiever, a caring and loving mother, a mature individual—an remarkable person—the last person you'd expect to react this way.

It's all too common that we make up stories about what we *think* will happen or what we *think* another person will do. When we create false narratives, aligning our actions with them, we shut down possibilities and are wasting time. Instead, we should be in our experience and benefit from the wisdom that presence offers.

Example. I had the fortunate opportunity to meet Eckhart Tolle. During his presentation at a conference, he told a story of the time he sent a copy of his book to Oprah for her endorsement. Weeks and months went by, and during that time he could have allowed his mind to take over, thinking, "She doesn't like my book. It's too early in my career to have sent it to her. I'll never make it as a writer. She's too big and doesn't have time for new authors." But he did not do this because none of these reactions were real. Eckhart was present with reality. The truth was she just didn't respond. He continued writing and focusing on his path. Oprah eventually responded by having him on her show and featuring his book, which became a huge success. Now, he has a relationship with her. The fact that he *did not* give his allegiance to a false narrative prevented him from experiencing severe anxiety and real suffering.

We leave the present moment and begin thinking about the past or the future. Debriefing to learn from past events and planning for what's next is necessary and smart. However, when we start to ponder events of the past by thinking, *I should have, I would have, I could have,* we leave the present moment. Similarly, if we ponder thoughts of *"What if it doesn't work?" "What if they don't like me?" "What if it rains?"* we're not experiencing the present moment. This dislocation happens frequently. Imagine being in a meeting and thinking about the meeting you just had or the next meeting. When this happens, instead of being present at the current moment, you are distracted.

We don't let our emotions flow in the present moment. By denying our emotions, we leave our current experience. This takes us out of presence. Avoiding feelings empowers our mind to be in charge. When we lose control of a situation, rather than letting our feelings flow, we create internal tension. Instead of using our feelings to our advantage, we believe that showing emotions means we are vulnerable and undesirable. We try to manage our emotional energy. It is with this management of our self that we leave the moment. We lose presence and cut off our natural capacities. We are so busy *managing* our experience that we *leave* our experience. Emotional intelligence is a practice you can master so that vulnerability will no longer be an issue for you.

We dive into technology to leave our current experience. There is a lot of discussion about technology and mindfulness. Some of these conversations maintain that social media and other technology platforms keep us from being connected. Technology is an extraordinary gift of advancement that has allowed us to accomplish a great many things as a species. But as remarkable as it is, it's just like anything else. When we fall into unconscious patterns, we leave the present moment. It is no different than a sport, meditation, or a social interaction. When we lose presence, we disconnect. When we use technology as an avoidance tactic, we are not present. When playing tennis, we must be present with our body, the racket, the court, the ball, etc. When we are not, we will trip, miss the backhand, or hit the ball into the net. It's the same with technology. If we are not present with our body, we may be avoiding rest and, instead, surfing the web. If we are not present with our keyboard, we may be making mistakes, taking longer to type, or sending an ineffective email. If we are not present with our location, we may be at our last meeting, even though it has ended, and scanning unconsciously through Facebook, Twitter, etc.

New studies show how technology can be an actual addiction. When we see that *like* on Facebook, or hear that *ding* alerting us to a new message or email, we experience a hit of dopamine. This becomes the addiction. We *want* that feeling; the addiction becomes the driver and not presence. This addiction is real and must be taken lightly, but it's just like every other bad habit. Technology is a gift. It is up to us to be present with it and conscious of how we use it, rather than blaming technology for polluting our experience.

These are just some of the ways we are not present; there are others. Presence is a practice and, as we practice, we will discover new ways that resonate with us that help us get back into flow.

CHAPTER 3

STOP *OUR* ADDICTION TO DRAMA

One of the common ways we drift from presence is when we avoid the appropriate level of responsibility because of our addiction to drama. We are not in the truth of who we are and don't respond with ability. We allow our ego to drive our behavior when we respond; we don masks or personas to hide our authentic, genuine self and create a dynamic called The Drama Triangle.[1,2,3]

The dynamic is so common, so prevalent in society that this chapter is called *our* addiction to drama. Individually and collectively, we can immediately increase the energetic vibration of our world by owning the truth that we are committed to drama.

The truth of who we are, not just some aspect of our personality, must be authentic, real, or genuine. When acting in alignment with what we stand for and who we are, not who someone says we should be, we're responding from a place of *being* real, authentic, and genuine.

Drama exists when our inner experience doesn't match our outer exterior. We spend most of our time letting our mind and ego get in the way by wearing a mask, an aspect of our personality called a persona. Instead of being true, we create our own movie, write the script in our mind, and play the leading or supporting role. This behavior aligns our activities around these personas. Even our postures change to meet the persona. We do this all day long. When playing these characters, we aren't in real connection, and we aren't optimizing for impact.

The three characters we play to create drama are Hero (aka rescuer), Victim, or Villain (aka persecutor). We are each responsible for our part in our activities and interactions. When we wear these masks, we take too much, too little, or no responsibility for our actions in the world.

When we lose presence by not owning our share of responsibility, we create drama, and internal and external conflict ensues. We can all relate to drama in the workplace; it is a productivity and connection killer. Ponder your interactions from drama versus presence.

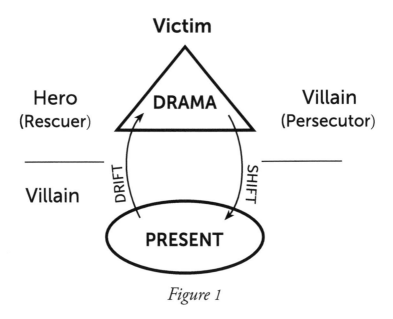

Figure 1

The Hero—Rescuing When It's Not Necessary

The Hero. Think of the Hero in terms of taking too much, too little, or no responsibility. When we take more than our share of responsibility, we become a rescuer—a Hero. The Hero looks for sources of suffering and assumes they can control the situation. In the Hero role, you're acting with expectations of a reward, or so you and others, because of your deeds, will *feel better*. The Hero plays this role by saving others who don't need to be saved. Heroes take responsibility for the *weight of the world.*

You are probably thinking of some Heroes with whom you work. These are the people who volunteer for extra projects and do more than their share. They don't believe that others can get it done, so they do it themselves. They don't know how to delegate; in fact, Heroes don't even think that *delegating* is an option. These are people who want to save the day, even though the day doesn't need to be saved.

Subscribing to the scenario that everyone needs to be saved, Heroes try to rescue and get involved unnecessarily. They also absorb responsibilities when they haven't been asked. The Hero is the person who attempts to do everything, becomes overwhelmed, and ends up with illness or burnout. They keep piling on more and more work, even though they don't have the capacity. Heroes strive to seek approval and love through *doing* while wearing the mask. Through all this *doing,* they are not mindful of their productivity, which always suffers.

This isn't to say we shouldn't be proactive, but we must assess our intent behind the action. To be present is to take responsibility for our part *and no more.* When we are wearing the mask of Hero, we want others to notice we are doing extra work. Instead, we can be present and recognize that others are available and able to function without having to rescue them.

Heroes have blind optimism, thinking that they can easily push a boulder up Mt. Everest while blind, naked, backwards, and without oxygen.

Consider this Hero: the former Wall Street executive who had such a strong desire to perform pushed herself to the limit. One day, she left her office in lower Manhattan to head home. Wearing a suit, heels, makeup, and with briefcase in hand, she realized she'd be late to catch the ferry. Without a thought, she puts it into high gear and starts running. She makes the ferry on time and, while sitting there, realizes *"Wow! Here I am in my suit and heels, and I just passed a runner!"* Two years later, the effects of pushing herself serve as a wake-up call. She suffered from headaches, neck pain, shoulder pain, hip pain, and, finally, shooting foot cramps in her feet and up her legs.

This former Wall Street executive is me—I am a *reformed* Hero. I would volunteer for everything and do *way* more than my share of work. Thinking I had to do it all, I dis-empowered others who wanted to step up, take responsibility, and contribute. What added to my suffering is that I have huge capacity, am a high performer, and very efficient. I perpetuated the egocentric pattern by not being able to discern productivity from rescuing. My actions prevented others from failing, and growing, and learning from their mistakes. Furthermore, I would burn out and get a cold twice a year, and of course, I wouldn't be absent when I was feeling ill because my colleagues *needed* me.

I have a client who had a very strong Hero pattern. He would take on so much work that his performance would suffer. His Hero pattern was such that during a workshop, he'd stop to ask the group if anyone needed anything to eat or drink, even though I explained that there would be breaks which included drinks and snacks. The workshop was about this very topic—drama. At the moment, my client and I could use it as an example of playing Hero. The entire group saw in action the disruption the Hero can create. In this case, it was a minor disruption of a workshop. This resonated with the other Heroes in the room, and they are now are using the skills in this book.

Another client, a brilliant designer at a social media company, consistently wears the Hero mask, feeling she must save the day and do more than her share of work. Thinking others are incapable, she doesn't transfer her technical expertise and wisdom to anyone else. Everyone looks to her as the expert that she is, and still, she struggles letting go of work. Overloaded and headed for burnout, she beats herself up for failing to keep up. This diminishes her ability to connect and make an impact and stifles others' potential. Heroes disempower others by not seeing them as capable and whole. They set up conditions which stifle others' opportunities to grow and develop.

From Heroes, you'll hear comments such as, *"I'll take care of it," "I can help," "Poor you," "I got this! I got this! Give it to me I can do it!" "Give it to me so that you can go be with your kids," "We can do this!" "Let me help you with that."*

The physical posture of a Hero is one of forward, nervous, frenetic energy, and high adrenaline. It's as if they are running on high octane all the time so that they can handle it *because no one else can.*

Once again, Heroes take more than their share of responsibility by saving the day when the day doesn't need to be saved.

The Victim—at the Effect of Everything

A second character we play is Victim. Victims take less than their share of responsibility. They play Victim by veiling awareness of their personal power and, in doing so, significantly diminish it. You are in the Victim mode if you are feeling overwhelmed or powerless. The Victim plays out their role through a declaration of pain and suffering, as well as defeat. These people are at the *effect* of everything and are waiting for someone else to fix the problem. These are the whiners of the world. If you find yourself whining, you are probably wearing the Victim mask.

Victims cannot find solutions. They are the dis-empowered leaders. Think about how inspiring someone is who is not in his or her power—not very. They will say things like, *"Our company just had a major re-organization so there is nothing we can do about this," "There's nothing I can do to be promoted," "I'll never be able to get ahead here with all the changes," "How am I supposed to lose weight when we have seven restaurants on campus?"*

The Victim plays out their role by admitting defeat from the beginning. *"There's nothing I can do,"* is a typical phrase used by a Victim. Instead of asking what *is* possible or what *can* be done, it's as if they're going into a tennis match they've already lost, so why even play? During a meeting, a Victim will think, *"Why participate? There's no reason for me to. Everyone else already has the answers."* The *it's not fair* mentality shows up. A Victim often feels misunderstood or undervalued.

Consider these examples. One client of mine wasn't promoted and started whining, *"This isn't fair. I will never get to Director."* He wasn't present with the truth of the situation and wasn't taking responsibility for neglecting to position himself for the promotion.

Another client with a strong preference for introversion wasn't speaking up in meetings. She was deep in Victim mode when she whined, *"I can't get a word in, so there's nothing I can do to get my ideas heard."*

My client, a Director of Research, plays Victim. An excellent connector of people, she is a subject matter expert. And yet when she's in a room of powerful personalities, she immediately shrivels up, becomes quiet, and will even flip-flop on her expert opinion. She comes across as very inconsistent and not in her power, lacking self-confidence. She plays Victim at the effect of these *powerful* people. Her colleagues wonder, *"Why doesn't she just speak up? Where did she go? Who is here now?"*

During my days in financial services, I witnessed mass Victim-hood when the firm I worked for, Merrill Lynch, was bought by Bank of America. All around me I heard, *"Why is this happening to us?"* Whenever you hear yourself ask this question, you are probably playing the Victim.

The Victim posture is the opposite of a power posture. It embodies a total lack of personal power and authority. Usually slumped and hunched over, Victims physically do not command or own the room and, instead, become part of the furniture, their presence isn't felt.

Victims take less than their share of responsibility—at the effect of everything and everyone.

The Villain—Placing Blame Outside of Self

The third character we play is Villain. Villains take zero responsibility and assign blame externally. It's everyone else's fault but theirs. They focus on a single convenient answer—to find and blame a scapegoat. You will know you are in the Villain persona if you feel your opinion is correct and only search for evidence that supports your claims. The Villain plays out their role by declaring that they *know* and are *right*, thus keeping attention on the problem and stifling open discussion. Villains are constant complainers.

As blamers and critics, they seek control. Villains will say, *"It's his fault this happened," "I just did what I was told," "We're doing it this way because that's what he says," "My manager is making me do this."* They blame or criticize someone else, taking zero responsibility for contributing to the situation. A Villain may even be neutral about blame and may not even comment, but are still taking zero responsibility for their contribution to the conditions they are creating. Consider these real-life Villains—the software engineer who can't delegate work because no one is competent enough to do it right, or the software designer who blames his dissatisfaction on *weird organizational conversations*. And then consider the female executive who complains because women can't get ahead. There's enough gender bias in the world without adding drama to it.

Here's another real situation. A highly competent Senior Vice President of a pharmaceutical company plays Villain. He easily becomes bored in meetings. His arms start to cross, and he glares at the people across the table. They immediately make up stories about his behavior and even wonder if they've done something wrong. The focus shifts from the agenda to what's happening with the dynamic in the room, a breakdown of productivity and connection. He is dissatisfied with how he shows up—he starts villainizing himself with internal mental chatter.

From Villains you will hear, *"It should be different," "You're wrong," "Bugger off!" "Well, I'm just doing what my manager said. I'm just doing what I'm told." "It's the way this company runs, we are never going to be able to get things done efficiently," "She's an idiot," "He doesn't know what he's doing," "Our team has issues."*

The observable posturing of a Villain is one of eye-rolling, arms crossed, critical treatment, and blaming others. They are the finger-pointers and usually wear scowling expressions with sarcastic or negative tones to their interactions. They take zero responsibility altogether and shift blame to others.

Heroes, Victims, and Villains—quite the set of characters—come together and create the Drama Triangle. When I see it happening in my workshops, it usually inspires laughter, but in a professional setting, it is not a laughing matter. (See Figure 1, The Drama Triangle)

Persona	Responsibility	Attitude
Hero	More than their share	Poor you + hyperactivity
Victim	Less than their share	Poor me + whining
Villain	Zero share	Bugger off! + complaining

These are the three common characters we play, but we don't necessarily play just one. We might have a foot in two, or even all three. These personas know no boundaries across cultures. You know what drama feels like—the mental swirl, the discussions that go nowhere, conflict that continues. While in drama, there exists *no real connection, no forward progress, no impact.* While this dynamic in groups is prevalent, we don't need others to get into drama. We create it all in our mind. We create the inner swirl of mind chatter.

The Drama Triangle in Action

You've seen The Drama Triangle. Someone is late to a meeting, so it doesn't start on time. The Villain will have an attitude of "It's her fault that we started late." By taking the Villain stance, they are neglecting their share of responsibility that they didn't ask to start the meeting. The late person, perhaps a Victim, will whine, "There are too many meetings for me to keep up with." A Hero at the same meeting will try to keep the peace and make up for the drama by taking on even more work to put people at ease. All three roles perpetuate the pattern and collude to keep drama in place—hence the addiction.

You've probably overheard conversations where people race for the Victim persona, often playing the game, "Who's the biggest Victim?" Conversations about commuting, frequent manager changes, or the current state of affairs easily turn to drama by people wanting to earn their place at the top of the Victim ranks.

Another example has to do with cultural changes in organizations. Many people blame (Villainize) their organization for cultural changes or are at the effect of (feel Victimized by) cultural changes. We forget that we all contribute to and have responsibility for any culture that exists. In fact, being conscious in every moment that we *are* the culture that is created is a big step into presence. Even as a consultant, I have responsibility for any company's culture as I interact with their employees.

Being in The Drama Triangle—When We Are Not Present

- Our ego is in charge
- We feel stuck and feel a chronic inability to get things done or move the ball forward
- We are maintaining or escalating conflict
- We are whining or complaining
- *Everything* is serious, and we have *zero* ability to laugh
- We aren't letting emotions flow, and we feel constricted
- We want to be right, and we argue every possible position to be right
- We are closed to other points of view by holding a position, thinking, *This is the way.*
- We are feeling righteous, and we are judging
- We are acting childish and immature
- Everyone feels like an enemy
- We are running on and are addicted to adrenaline

- We have shallow breath or aren't breathing, and our posture is locked

When we stop breathing, our physiology is fighting us. Our lungs fill with CO_2, and we start to produce adrenaline. We then go into The Drama Triangle and become unconscious of our actions. Our conditioned patterns are in charge, and we are on autopilot. This state is not sustainable. After the adrenaline wears off, we feel drained. In seeking that adrenaline fix again, our ego takes over. We stop breathing, adrenaline kicks in, and we are back into drama. This is the roller-coaster/hamster-wheel experience of interacting from personas. Our ego perpetuates the conditions to keep the pattern running, thereby locking down any innovative, collaborative energy that exists. A repeated theme in this book addresses supporting the nervous system by bringing more attention to our bodies.

We Don't Need Others to Participate in The Drama Triangle

Our ego in conflict isn't just an outer expression. This dynamic also happens in our minds. We may not be in drama with someone else, but with ourselves. Inwardly criticizing ourselves and beating ourselves up are common examples of internal drama. It's common for even the most successful and powerful people to have inner drama. I remember playing the Hero, offering to take on more work. I became tired and fell into Victim mode by being at the effect of my activities. Then, I would kick myself in the behind to pick up the pace to *get over it and get the job done* and along comes my Hero to save the day—in this case, to save myself—to get going again.

There is *zero* transformational value in villainizing ourselves. The ego becomes comfortable sustaining patterns and uncomfortable when creating new paradigms. The simple solution here is to notice the drift from presence and choose consciously to be present. Spending time beating ourselves up is completely unnecessary and takes us further into drama, where real suffering occurs.

Why Do We Lose Presence and Create Drama?

Why do we do it? Why are we addicted to drama? Think about friends and colleagues. This doesn't make sense for intelligent professional people wanting to make an impact. We all have a strong desire to perform, to be excellent, to be connected. Why in the world would any of us put on a mask and act in any way other than authentically, who we are? Because we are human beings. We have formed habits and patterns of behavior. The same way we form tactical habits to get through our day-to-day, we create behavioral habits. We go on autopilot. We get into routines and are unaware of ourselves—we are unconscious. Now is the time to wake up. Raise your consciousness and your collective consciousness and learn how to become a conscious and evolved human being and leader. Be present.

Common Reasons for Drifting to Drama

Adrenaline. We create drama to get an adrenaline hit. At some point, we start to rely on adrenaline to get through our day. We work in fast-paced environments. Most of us aren't breathing deeply into our bellies. Our body goes on alert and produces adrenaline. Soon enough, we aren't aware that we are relying on it for everything.

Adrenaline is a very addictive drug. When people initially experience it being released in their body, it feels highly uncomfortable. A feeling of panic occurs when it floods the system, body, and mind, and leads to further production. This significant release of adrenaline can cause us to become conditioned to it or need it for normal functioning. After months of this, people often come to love the edge that this fix gives them in terms of energy, mood boost, and quick wit. But too much adrenaline can lead to health issues such as high blood pressure, heart attack, physical pain, excessive anxiety, and hypochondria.

I can relate to the adrenaline addiction. I played the Hero to get the adrenaline rush. I took on more work than was necessary. I was on every extra project. I worked weekends. I got three to four hours of sleep a night. I didn't take care of myself. The long-term effects of adrenaline were what caused my body pain. With conscious awareness, I overcame the addiction and reset my body's natural state of homeostasis.

There might be a time when adrenaline is useful. Life is not easy, and we have goals to meet. We may need a hit of adrenaline to get through the day or week. That's okay if it's used consciously. But relying on it to get through day-do-day activity is not sustainable.

To be right. Our ego *wants* to be right. We love to challenge others, but when someone challenges us, we don't like it. On goes our protective mask, we drop out of reality and create drama, justifying our point of view from any one of the roles, and remaining in the right, holding our position versus looking for a win for all.

Entertainment. Drama is very entertaining, hence the addiction. These dynamics are fun to watch on movies or TV. We are *doers,* and if we aren't *doing,* we get unsettled, so we seek out entertainment with our colleagues in the form of drama. We get the adrenaline hit. We are entertained. And we get to argue. When we're finished with short-term entertainment, we realize we haven't made any progress.

Avoid the unknown. Drama helps us avoid the unknown, which can be very scary. We don't know what's going to happen in technology other than we know it will change. An individual may not know what's going to happen during their performance review. They may not be sure what's going to happen with the outcome of a project or may not know the trajectory of their career. Instead of letting ourselves be in the unknown, fear takes over, causing us to put on a mask and play Hero, Victim or Villain. The roles are known.

Avoid emotions. We by-pass our emotions and create drama. Emotions can be very uncomfortable. Emotional *intelligence* is crucial to leadership and being a human being, but at the same time, we aren't comfortable with our feelings. To avoid feeling fear, sadness, anger, even joy, we step into drama. Instead of consciously feeling our emotions, we unconsciously replace them with the hit of adrenaline. Feeling emotions puts us in a vulnerable place, and it's not easy. What's easier is to avoid our feelings, and cover them up with a persona. Then no one can know our inner experience. We hide behind the persona.

Maintain control. We create drama when we become afraid of losing control. Our ego likes to be in charge and in control of others. This is another illusion. "If only you would be different and do what I say, my work would be so much easier." The reality is that there is very little we can control. As much as we'd like to control others and our circumstances, it is not possible.

When we feel out of control, our body is on alert and goes into a fear state. Our sympathetic nervous system is activated as if there is a predator. Our bodies pump adrenaline and cortisol into our veins, sending us directly into drama. The reality is instead of being truthful about our fear of not being in control; we wear a mask so our mind can manipulate the situation and create the illusion that we are protected and in control. It's not *real* control—it's *perceived* control.

Avoid difficult conversations and confrontations. Gossip is full of drama. Instead of getting present and having difficult conversations, we go behind others' backs and gossip. This is not flattering. Instead of being present and telling the truth, we avoid a hard conversation and put on a mask, instigating drama. This gives the impression that we are making forward progress when we are in an unproductive swirl. When gossiping, we are interacting from The Drama Triangle.

Autopilot. One of the simplest reasons we put on a mask is habit. We're on autopilot, falling into the trap of an old pattern that once was of service. Behavioral habits are helpful and can be useful, but if left uninvestigated, we are not in charge of our experience. Autopilot is unconscious. In the absence of conscious commitments, awareness, and activities, our unconscious patterns—such as group think, when groups follow along with each other unconsciously—rule us. Running on autopilot keeps us from adapting to the moment, avoiding the truth, pain, and discomfort of that moment.

These are just some of the reasons we are attracted to drama. A few examples can be seen in the following descriptions of executives.

One client, who is conscious of his Hero persona, said to me, "I'm addicted to adrenaline. I keep going for the rush." Another, ensconced in a chair across from me, slumped down and said, "I'm just not in my leadership potential." He was in Victim mode, fearing not being in his full potential. A senior executive who lost presence became bored, crossed his arms, and shut down, wearing the Villain mask. Playing out the Villain persona assures him he's right. Another example is the client who takes on the Villain role with one of her employees, blaming her for not being able to keep up for fear of losing control over the project.

These examples are of individuals who are exceptional, caring, achieving professionals who want to make a difference. By noticing how we drift into drama and consciously choosing to shift back into presence, we can take our leadership to the next level.

Getting Present

There is an alternative that is always available. It is the natural state—presence. Conscious leaders know that presence is the most impactful gift that can be given. Presence is always available.

Example. We're in a state of presence and something happens. Usually, all it takes is for someone else to walk into the room.

We drop our awareness and leave presence. Our persona takes over and movie/illusion starts. We drift into drama.

Notice where you are. Recognize the characteristics when you are Hero, Victim, or Villain. When in the Hero persona, you may begin to talk faster, your voice becomes higher, and you may be filled with nervous, negative energy. Feel the adrenaline as if you're plugged into an electrical socket. When in Villain, your arms may be crossed, you may be dismissive, hardly listening, and thinking, "Speed this up!" Victim mode is accompanied by subtle whining, thinking, "It's not worth it," or "Why bother?"

Become familiar with these characteristics—this is your dharma bell. When you drift, you *can* shift back to presence. (Figure 1)

Start immediately. No delay. Go directly to presence. It is always available to you. Again, it is your natural state.

Come back to presence with Shift Moves. These concepts are very simple, but not easy. If you are looking for a complex formula here, you won't find it. You have a full life, so keep it simple.

Shift Moves Lead to Presence

Notice the drift from presence. This is simple but powerful. By noticing you are not present, this will bring you back into the present moment. This is a moment-by-moment conscious choice to recognize if you are in the present moment or not. As your awareness increases, you can become masterful by noticing you are drifting from presence and, instead of losing presence, you are mindful and able to stay present. This takes practice. Once you recognize your drift from presence, use one of the following Shift Moves to return to presence.

Breathe. Simple. Make sure you are breathing into your belly. This sounds easy, but surprisingly, it's not. Most of us maintain a shallow breath. Our lungs fill with CO_2. Our sympathetic nervous system is always engaged on a low hum. Adrenaline and cortisol are pumped through the body, creating drama. The brain uses twenty percent of the oxygen in the body, three times more than muscles. You need and want your brain at work to carry out your day-to-day activities. If you are not getting sufficient oxygen, your body is on alert; alarms are going off. Practicing deep breathing trains your body to relax. By doing so, you will be flooding your cognition and your physiology with oxygen. The body and brain need it to function effectively.

Move. Move your body, and change your posture. Each of the roles has a posture. The patterns become locked in our muscular tensions, in our physiology. By changing your body's posture, you interrupt your muscular tension—your pattern. Become familiar with your postures and move differently to break the pattern. The importance of movement has been known since the 1970s, and there is a new body of science coming out now regarding the importance of movement and posture. Studies show long periods of sitting are more detrimental then smoking. Move your body! If you pay attention to your posture and change it up regularly, you will be less likely to be pulled into drama.

Breathing and moving are the most effective Shift Moves to presence. The next time you're in a meeting and tensions are running high; everyone is in drama, I dare you to say, "Let's stop, everyone. Let's take a big breath, get up and move, shake it off." You will be delightfully shocked at the difference. The energy in the room will change dramatically. When the symptoms of drama appear, the first thing to ask is, "Am I breathing into my belly?" Yes, or no. If *no*, start breathing. If *yes*, then change your posture and try other Shift Moves.

Tell the truth. This Shift Move is self-inquiry which is the invitation to tell the truth, investigate and ask yourself, "What's going on here? What's up with me? Is this me speaking or thinking, or is a persona in charge?" This is what self-inquiry is, being honest with yourself and telling the truth.

Example. You're sitting in a meeting. You begin to think, *We have been talking about the same topic now for the last forty-five minutes. We have five more items on the agenda and fifteen minutes left. We are never going to get to all of them. These people are idiots!* You have just drifted to drama.

Here's what I *don't* mean by telling the truth. "Abby says we should tell the truth, so I want to tell you that this meeting is dragging on and you all are idiots." Let me be clear: that's not what I mean! I mean: you can investigate, "What's going on with me?" The *truth*, what's going on, is I am avoiding stating the meeting which isn't productive, and I just took on the role of Villain.

Self-inquiry is an invitation to presence because you are in the truth that you've been hijacked by a persona. From there, you are more present with yourself and may speak or not speak from a place of presence. You have choices. So instead of stewing silently in a Villain persona, you may speak up. *"I want to stop everyone. I'm noticing we've been talking about this one topic for forty-five minutes. We still have five more items on the agenda with only fifteen minutes left. What do you think?"* Or you may even choose not to speak up, but you've told the truth to yourself, that you drifted to Villain and at least *you* will be more attentive. Self-inquiry is a powerful Shift Move—tell the truth to yourself about what's going on. This can bring you back to presence. The next Shift Move works well when you are in conflict.

Appreciation. Stop and appreciate anything. Appreciate yourself for noticing that you are creating drama. Appreciate others for being with you while you are not present. Appreciate that you *can* stop and appreciate. Appreciation is a shift to positive energy that is inherently a shift from conflict. Stop and appreciate anything. Appreciate yourself that you are participating, and appreciate your colleagues for hanging in there with you during this conflict or tough conversation. Appreciate the intensity of the conflict itself and that you have a comfortable chair to sit in while it's happening. When you start to bring appreciation into the experience, conflict will begin to diffuse. With appreciation, there is a better chance that the dynamic in the room will change.

Let your emotions flow. You lose presence when you come out of emotional flow by resisting this energy, these feelings in your body. To deny your emotions is to deny the truth of your experience. Welcome your feelings, and you will be more present. (See Emotional Intelligence)

Be in your experience. Notice what is right in the moment. It can be anything. "I'm noticing I am resisting the truth. I'm aware I am following the narrative of my mind. I am aware that I have a headache. I feel my arms resting on this chair. I'm holding my breath. I want to blame someone." Being with what is here, right now, will get you present.

Bring love and compassion to yourself—just the way you are. We all experience conditioned patterns that overcome us and keep us from being present with ourselves and others. The ability to love and show compassion for yourself is a powerful way to become present. With unconditional self-love and compassion, you can be with any truth that arises and makes conscious choices going forward that are of more service to you and others.

Notice what you are avoiding or seeking. We frequently leave the current moment to avoid something, someone, or some experience. Often, when we are seeking something, we reach out to technology and social media, seeking connection from external sources rather than the connection with our self that is *always* available. The Shift Move here is to notice what you are avoiding, and to speak or take direct action toward what you want.

Play and exaggerate your current attitude. This is especially effective if you are serious. Have fun with your personas and exaggerate your behavior. If you are in Victim, at the effect of something, you can make that big by exaggerating it. Many of us can relate to being stuck in traffic on the way to work. You may be playing a Victim role and shift by exaggerating this attitude. *"Oh my, I'm never going to get to work. At this rate, I'll get to work in a year!"* When I facilitate team workshops. I invite people to don the mask they typically wear and then hold a team meeting. They are amazed at the time they spend in drama. When you notice the hilarity, it brings levity to the whole situation. That will get you present and out of drama.

An example of shifting to presence. I taught this framework to a client, a board of directors. They were at their board meeting, and I was facilitating The Drama Triangle. During the exercise, two people from the board created drama. One of them, Jane, was villainizing me as the facilitator, blaming me for the dysfunction of the group. I asked her if she was willing to experiment. She resisted at first but then agreed. Another board member across the room, Dave, said, "I'll experiment with you." He also created drama. The two of them came to the front of the room. I asked Jane to explain what was happening for her. She verbally villainized me in front of the group. I jumped in and intentionally stepped into an exaggerated Villain role and said, "Well, it's *your* fault. You're not listening." Dave joined in as Hero and said, "Come on, can't you get along?" I became present again, and Dave and Jane continued in a battle of personas. Finally, having drifted from Villain to exaggerated Victim, Jane turned to me and said, *"You* made us do this." With that, Jane started laughing because she realized she was caught up in extreme drama. The others in the room were laughing, too. Suddenly she said, "Yeah, I get it. I'm wasting a lot of energy." The group could easily see the potential impact of re-channeling the energy from drama to instead make an impact on the world. They now pay attention when their personas take over. They pay attention to when they are present or not present. They notice what triggers them to go into drama and the conditions they create. They are playing and practicing Shift Moves from drama to presence. This simple, yet powerful, real-world business example shows how the practice of presence can influence the bottom line. What could this practice of presence do for your business and relationships?

Evolve via Practice

Our persona takes over, and we act from one mask to the other, perhaps even wearing more than one mask at the same time. This is okay. The goal is to notice when the drift from presence occurs, and shift back. The measure of success is how quickly the gap is closed from when you drifted to presence and shifted back. That's it. And you must practice. If you don't, nothing will change, and you will continue to create drama.

Drama Begets Drama—Presence Begets Presence

The Drama Triangle is very entertaining and adrenaline is addictive, so it is very tempting to take your attention away from yourself and start pointing out roles in others. But by doing so, you invite more drama. *Do not do this!*

You will have a bigger impact by focusing on yourself. Put the oxygen mask on first. Shift yourself out of drama and get present. It's difficult to be in drama around someone who is present. Similarly, it's difficult to get present around someone who is in drama. This is where it gets tricky. If you're in a meeting with four people who are in drama, it's difficult not to join them, but focus on staying present and don't get pulled into it. Drama begets drama.

Another temptation is to start judging yourself and others for creating drama. Instead of good/bad or right/wrong, just inquire, "Where am I, and what are the consequences?" Your interactions will be different when you are present versus drama. There is zero transformational value in beating yourself up for drifting to The Drama Triangle.

- Become knowledgeable
- Build the skill by practicing
- Become masterful

From mastery, you proactively start to invite others into presence. Until you are masterful, you run the risk of being pulled into drama. Put the oxygen mask on yourself. Start here first.

Self-Mastery—What Can Presence Do for Our Culture?

We must have agility. Technology is moving at such a rapid pace of innovation; we must keep up our own growth and evolution. It is evolving faster than we are, so we must raise our consciousness and evolve as human beings to be able to meet the demands of an ever-changing moment. What is required of you is a commitment to wake up, be conscious, and be present.

Instead of blaming, shaming, criticizing, and villainizing others, be an expert at relating to others. Conscious leaders and conscious people are needed so that we may collaborate, connect, contribute, and create wins for all situations.

In interactions with your colleagues, you can't get it done by yourself. Business brings us together. We can get more done with others versus alone. That's why companies are formed. That's why we come together in groups. We have a strong desire to perform. We want to connect with our colleagues and need to get present and welcome the truth, no matter what it is. When we are present, we align our actions around reality ,and we save time, enhance innovation, and experience infinite vitality. The experience of yourself and others will be real; authenticity cannot be faked. Presence is not wearing the mask. The mask is the illusion.

The real you is presence. You will bring what's required to the moment because you are smart and brilliant. You are connecting with others and can face anything. You don't have all the answers, but you can navigate anything with grace, power, professionalism, and compassion. You are more productive and have more fun. From presence, create real connection, real impact, and we all win.

What mask are *you* wearing?

Applying the Practice—Presence and The Drama Triangle

Step 1: Notice the drift from presence

Step 2: Close the gap and choose a Shift Move

Step 3: Apply the Shift Move

Step 4: Experience presence, and capture the wisdom of your direct experience

CREDIT ———————————————————

1 Karpman Drama Triangle. (n.d.). Retrieved August 16, 2014, from Wiki: http://en.wikipedia.org/wiki/Karpman_drama_triangle

2 Karpman MD, Stephen B. (2007). The New Drama Triangles USATAA/ITAA conference lecture August 11, 2007, Free Download Worksheet for the DVD. Retrieved from www.karpmandramatriangle.com

3 The Drama Triangle, a collaboration of the Hendricks Institute: www.hendricks.com and the Conscious Leadership Group: www.conscious.is

CHAPTER 4

THE MINDFULNESS MOVEMENT

The mindfulness movement is a part of popular culture. The term made it to the cover of *Time Magazine* in 2014 and was the main topic on an episode of *60 Minutes.* Entire workshop series and conferences are centered on it. Mindfulness solicits the question, "Shouldn't meditation help us empty our minds?" The process itself offers clarity on the value of incorporating it and practices based on mindfulness.

Mindfulness

Jon Kabat-Zinn, creator of the Center for Mindfulness in Medicine, says, "Mindfulness means paying attention in a particular way; on purpose, in the present moment, and non-judgmentally."[1] Much of the current day discussion of mindfulness is inspired by the teachings of the eastern world, particularly from the Buddhist traditions. There is a movement to bring mindfulness to organizations, particularly in the form of meditation.

Mindfulness increases our ability to see things as they arise clearly and without judgment. It facilitates both focusing and widening our attention as we become aware of ourselves and the world around us. The goal is to be more fully present in our lives.[2] A meditation practice helps us train our minds to be quiet, not to stray, and to stay focused.

Comparing meditation with conscious practices, imagine spending a day at the beach, sitting quietly on the shore meditating. When you are finished meditating, you decide to go for a swim, applying consciousness skills to ride the tide, navigate currents, and respond to any waves. Unable to predict the size of the waves, you know you can't control the water, but conscious practices help you navigate your experience and your relationship to the water. Your experience is more intense now that you are *in* the water. Some waves may be small, making it easy to float on a raft. Other waves may be so huge that you are overcome, and the wave takes you where it will. Meditation can help ground and prepare you for your swim. Consciousness skills help you while you are *in* the water.

Now, bring this analogy to the workplace, relationships, and life. Meditation helps strengthen your mind in preparation for interactions with others (prepping to go for a swim). Consciousness practices help when you are interacting with others (riding the waves). This is where life is challenging. It's one thing to sit on quietly on the beach, be still and breathe. It's a whole different experience to dive into a very active surf. With over forty thousand hours of leading teams and groups, I have learned that people struggle most with their interaction with others—*riding the waves*—and in getting along with others, especially in work and intimate relationships.

Do you *have* to meditate? No. Some people who have meditated every day for years still struggle when collaborating with others. Others, who meditate once a week, have recounted how it has changed their lives. Mindfulness and meditation itself can become a distraction, a drift from presence. If you are conscious of yourself and can recognize when your thoughts have been hijacked, then you may not need to meditate. So, experiment. Given the advancements in neuroscience, there is a great deal of evidence that points to real benefits from meditation. (Note: MBSR—Mindful Based Stress Reduction I meditate. My teacher, Gangaji, said it powerfully, "Meditation is just good hygiene."

There is a massive amount of information available on mindfulness and meditation. Do your own research, and you will discover there are many types of contemplative practices. Some have a specific focus such as building concentration, one-pointed awareness, or a relationship with a higher power. If meditation doesn't light you up, explore other contemplative practices that will allow you to increase your well-being. Only you know what will work for you. If you are not sure of that, stop, be still, and meditate.

CREDIT ─────────────────────────────

1 Retrieved from: www.mindfulnet.org/page2.htm

2 http://www.umassmed.edu/cfm/mindfulness-based-programs/faqs-mbsr-mbct/

CHAPTER 5

EMOTIONAL INTELLIGENCE 101

A consistent characteristic of conscious leaders is that they possess the maturity to navigate their emotions. No matter the topic—facilitating or coaching—inevitably the question arises "Where do emotions fit into this? My response? *"Everywhere!"* When I ask groups to, "Raise your hand if you think emotions are a part of being a human,and if you think emotional intelligence in the workplace is necessary and a non-negotiable trait," all hands go up. Then I say, "Raise your hand if you are comfortable feeling your emotions." Zero hands go up. I've experienced groups who laugh out loud at this juxtaposition and are so uncomfortable, they squirm in their seats. Sometimes I hear, "I don't know what to do when others are emotional." The healthiest thing you can do is *feel* your feelings and be present with others while they feel theirs. Being with your emotions is a skill, and you can be a master.

People are beginning to realize that the old paradigm *"There's no place for emotions in the workplace"* is outdated. No longer are we pressured to check our emotional bags at the door when we walk into the office. The research is vast and is still growing about the benefits of being emotionally intelligent and the link between stress and illness. When we don't let our emotional energy flow, we are putting undo stress on our nervous system. This can sometimes lead to a physical illness and can be a tough experience. With a strong nervous system, you create a strong life.

The underdeveloped emotional intelligence of people in the workforce demolishes innovation, growth, and connection. We can no longer think of emotions as having less validity than cognitive abilities; instead, see them as productive signals of wisdom that inform our cognitive process. Use your emotions to translate information into actionable experiences. Emotions inform our decision-making and how we travel through the world. When we ignore them, we are discounting volumes of wisdom. Furthermore, when we deny our feelings, we deny the truth of our experience, and our self-esteem inevitably takes a hit.

To bring even more clarity to the topic of emotional intelligence, we need to address vulnerability and empathy.

Vulnerability can be defined as being in a state where one is easily hurt or harmed physically, mentally, or emotionally; open to attack, harm, or damage."[1]

Everyone is vulnerable and open to moral and physical attacks at times; our nervous systems are *extremely* vulnerable. We are always open to physical, mental, and emotional harm, as well as moral criticism. Our actions and the actions of others can be harmful. No human being is immune to this. Our systems and organizations are also vulnerable because of advancements in technology. Many companies are vulnerable to becoming outdated in the blink of an eye.

It's important to discern vulnerability versus emotional intelligence. Vulnerability is not an emotion; it is a state. When we agree that we are all vulnerable—within this context— then we can become masters of emotional intelligence. You've heard, "I want him to be more vulnerable," or "She doesn't show enough vulnerability." This is usually the ultimate of projections, wanting someone else to show their emotions when it is YOU who wants permission to emote. It's time to wear our hearts on our sleeves because to be seen emoting is to experience our collective vulnerability. From here we can experience deep empathy.

Empathy can be described as the action of understanding, being aware of, being sensitive to, and vicariously experiencing the feelings, thoughts, and experiences of another of either the past or present without having the feelings, thoughts, and experiences fully communicated in an objectively explicit manner."[2]

We cannot have empathy for another if we are not aware of our own feelings. To have empathy for another, and to have empathy for others' vulnerabilities, we must be aware of and experience our own emotions fully. You know what it's like to be around someone who is emotionally fluent. They aren't engaging in an internal wrestling match, and you feel relaxed and safe around them.

When I returned from a 45-day leave from work, I took time off to help my father. Sadly, he passed away after a fight with dementia. I was in a team meeting and experienced a wave of emotion, a bit of sadness. I started to tear up just a little bit and, right away, someone said, "Okay, the meeting's over." The room cleared. I wasn't sobbing. Just a few tears were falling on my cheek.

I was amazed at the team's reaction. This experience was one of the factors that motivated me to teach emotional intelligence. No one was comfortable with my emotional experience, nor did they have the capacity to navigate their own experience in witnessing my sadness. I was fully present with my emotions, as well as the business topic being discussed. There was no need to stop the meeting.

Most people are mystified, even terrified of their own emotional energy, and try to classify emotions as either good or bad. Feelings are neither good nor bad. There are many judgments about anger, fear, and stigmas that come with emoting. Furthermore, anger, sadness, fear, or sexual feelings get closeted if people haven't learned emotional fluency. We witness people feeling angry and, instead of expressing that anger, they act out or are passive-aggressive. Why? Because they have not been taught how to be *with* and how to *directly experience* their feelings.

How to Be Emotionally Intelligent

Learn to accept emotions as a natural part of being a human being. This is a direct support of our nervous system functioning properly. Emotions are powerful indicators that we are alive, and life force energy is moving through us. By resisting our feelings, we separate from our experience. If repressed, our emotional energy can build up and come out in an unconscious or harmful way. When accepted and felt, it will pass through in moments. "Having a bad day" is a phrase that is no longer applicable.

Emotions come and go. Feelings are waves of energy, a psychosomatic experience. The energy appears in the form of feelings, sensations in our body, an emotion. Once we learn how to discern these feelings, we can use this wisdom to our advantage and incorporate feelings into our conversations when we connect with others.

How to Directly Experience Feelings

We are in an emotional state in every moment. Most intense emotional states last about ninety seconds and, sometimes, especially in intense situations such as grief, the emotional waves may come one after another. Navigate through your emotions and capture the wisdom of your feelings.

Step 1: Recognize the sensations in your body. As I mentioned, emotions are feelings, sensations in our body. It's crucial to wake up and understand the connection between the mind and the body. Most people believe that our brains cause our emotions when it's the other way around. Our body sensations are the emotions. To be familiar with what you are feeling, you must begin with your body by identifying the actual sensations you are feeling. This is hard for people to grasp—we are a very "in our thoughts" society. For example, I don't sing because I'm joyful. I'm joyful because I sing. The body experience creates the emotion. The complex connection between our neurology, endocrine systems, and immune systems leave no separation between mind and body. The thought, I am joyful, is a thought, it's not real. What's real are the feelings and sensations in our body, which in turn create a joyous experience. Try it out right now. Start smiling and you will notice you start to feel happy.

Step 2: Identify what emotion you are feeling. Once you identify your body sensations, you can become aware of what emotion you are experiencing. Each body sensation creates an emotion, a specific feeling. Smiling is associated with joy. Joy emanates from the body's sensation of smiling.

Step 3: Capture the wisdom from your feelings. Because our mind, body, brain, immune and endocrine systems are all connected, we can capture real wisdom from emotions. Each emotion has information from which you can choose to express or not to express freely and professionally.

Step 4: Breathe and move to support your nervous system and to keep your energy flowing. Your nervous system needs oxygen to function, and by breathing and moving, emotional waves come and go naturally.

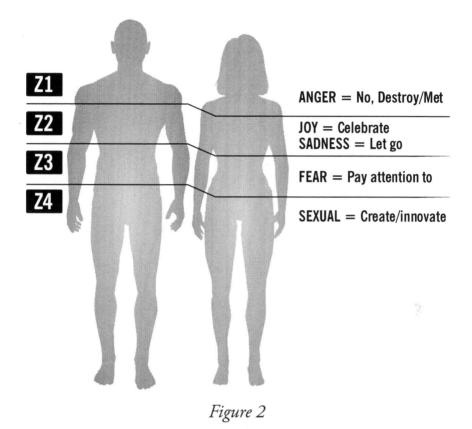

Z1

Z2

Z3

Z4

ANGER = No, Destroy/Met

JOY = Celebrate
SADNESS = Let go

FEAR = Pay attention to

SEXUAL = Create/innovate

Figure 2

Five Core Emotions

To begin to understand and experience true emotional intelligence, it's easiest to break down the experience into one or more of five core emotions. Remember that emotion begins *in your body*.

Anger. Typically, we feel anger in our body—head, neck, shoulders, and jaw. Symptoms range from tightness in our jaw, neck, and shoulders to a light or a severe headache. Some peoples' faces turn red when they are angry. When we feel angry, there's some *No* that wants to be expressed. It creates healthy boundaries and is an excellent use of resistance energy.

Wisdom. Anger is an indication that something wants to be met head-on. I felt angry with a colleague when he didn't complete his part in alignment with our agreement. I chose to express this professionally and told him I was angry and didn't feel met in our agreement. I asked him if he wanted to explain why he hadn't completed his part of the project. He didn't have a plausible reason. Since expressing my anger, my feelings, he completes tasks on time.

Not every situation will have this kind of positive result, but it's critical that we express our feelings professionally, without attachment to another person's experience. When we don't perform in alignment with our level of knowledge, experience, preparation, and wisdom, we are not in alignment with who we are and we will feel angry about our performance.

Anger may be telling us it's time to destroy. Destruction is an important part of the evolutionary continuum. We may feel anger at how people treat each other; time to *destroy* old ways of interacting and channel anger in productive ways. Until we evolve to a new level of maturity, we will continue to interact from drama. Destroy old stories about feelings, and become emotionally intelligent. You may continue to feel angry until this happens.

Many people categorize anger as bad or negative. How can having boundaries be bad? They are very important in thriving on a personal level and a professional one. Change the perception immediately that anger is negative. What is harmful and bad is when we don't meet our anger and consciously experience it. Instead, we attack others. Next time you're working on a project, and someone is angry, ask them, "What do you have a *No* for? What are you seeing that we're doing on this project that we shouldn't be doing?" And if you're feeling angry, ask yourself, "What do I have a *No* for?"

Be masterful at learning how to channel anger productively, especially when collaborating with others. If you disagree with something that is happening, or things don't go your way, you may feel anger. Learn how to move your energy forward even though it may not be consistent with what you think.

Technology is changing virtually everything. Many of the projects we work on with others are brand new and innovative. Everyone will have an idea about how energy should be implemented, but it's not always possible to use all the ideas every time. This may cause anger that it's not being done *your* way. That's okay, but when you leave the room, be united with your colleagues and channel anger energy to something productive. All of this is easier said than done and requires discipline and strength.

Joy. Joy usually presents an overall expanse of pleasant sensations, often emanating from the chest. Smiling does initiate joy.

> ***Wisdom.*** Joy is the call to celebrate. Most people know how to experience joy and are comfortable with feeling it. We experience joy by laughing together, smiling, allowing the pleasant energy to flow easily through our bodies. A very typical way to share joy is Happy Hour, expressing wins, acknowledging a successful product launch or promotion.

Sadness. Sadness typically starts in our chest and is a heavy feeling. Often, the throat will constrict and cause the eyes to tear.

> ***Wisdom.*** Sadness is a signal there is something that needs to be released. A universal example of this is death. When a loved one passes away, we may experience a heavy feeling, most often in the chest. We feel sad and may cry. This is a part of releasing the deceased. Most people are familiar with this experience.

In the workforce, this may look like a project that we decide to scrap because it may not be in the company's best interest. You might have a sense of loss over this project. It may not bring you to tears, but you may have a heavy chest and feeling of sadness.

One client just launched new software he created. He performed extraordinarily well and spoke of it at a meeting with his colleagues. Then he turned it over to other engineers to maintain. This was our dialog.

Abby: "What's bugging you?"

Client: "I have those post-launch blues."

Abby: "I heard the launch went well. Do you feel sad?"

Client: "I do, but I shouldn't."

Abby: "Why not? You feel happy, too. Correct?"

Client: "Yes."

Abby: "You've poured your heart and soul into the launch and feel sad to turn it over to others. Time to let go. But it's also time to celebrate. The launch went well. Can you see how these emotions are neither good nor bad? They just are."

Client: "I do."

The next day I received an email. "I feel great today. I went home last night, relaxed, and let myself feel sad. I let go of the project and am ready for something new. In the past, I would have wasted weeks stewing about it."

Sadness is normal. Most people skip over it and hold on to the project, rather than letting this energy flow naturally to make time for something new to be created. Overriding sadness is unhealthy and a challenge to the nervous system.

The next time someone around you is holding back tears, get present and tell them, "Let it flow!" Tears are not a sign of weakness, but an easy flow of energy and emotion.

Sexual. Sexual feelings emanate from the pelvis and can expand upward or downward. When experiencing these feelings, tingles may run up and down the legs.

> *Wisdom.* Our sexual energy is asking what to create or innovate. Ignoring sexual energy is common, as the topic of sex is often taboo. At home, there is another reason for sexual energy—sex. Of course, we should not walk around the office saying, "I feel

sexual." This is clearly unacceptable. But conscious leaders can discern between sexual *energy* and sexual *desire*. Sexual energy flow in the workplace is useful and does not require acting on sexual desire. Come into harmony with the useful life force of *sexual energy* by accepting the experience, while at the same time being smart and professional with your behavior.

Whenever a client says, "I feel frustrated," they may think they need a creative or innovative outlet. A hundred percent of the time, the answer is *No*. To consciously capitalize on this energy flow, act *toward* something creative and innovative. This may look like starting a brainstorming session, redesigning something, or creating something new altogether.

A client recently told me she was feeling frustrated. Our conversation went as follows:

Abby: "How do you let your creative energy flow? What creative activities do you partake in throughout your day?

Client: "I don't have any."

Abby: "Brainstorm, either alone or with friends, and start drawing on the walls of your office or doodle on a piece of paper—anything to get energy flowing."

She began exploring her creativity; she is no longer frustrated. (Note: the client works at a technology company where I am happy to say that many of the walls are whiteboards or chalkboards, so writing on walls is encouraged.)

Creative energy may be an indicator that it's time to challenge yourself. Whenever someone on the team becomes bored, it is a signal to start learning something new or push a new growth edge. It doesn't mean we must uproot everything and create chaos. Simple daily changes can insure effective and enjoyable channeling of energy, and innovative ideas are born.

Fear. Fear generates these kinds of responses. "I have butterflies in my belly" or "My stomach is in knots." When feeling fear, the belly constricts and you are not consciously breathing into your belly.

Wisdom. The wisdom behind fear is there's something that wants to attention. Fear is an invitation to be alert, see, notice, and take productive action.

A client was working on a very high-profile project and felt scared. She needed to *breathe.* Her action list included how to pay attention to her effectiveness during the project. She wanted to be sure her brand was intact during meetings and make certain she dotted her *i*'s and crossed her *t*'s.

With a promotion, a new project, or when you're poised on the edge of your next learning experience, some may fear energy. This is a call to be clear about what to focus on within yourself while you expand in your career. Fear is *momentum* energy designed to put us into action. Consciously experience fear rather than allow fear patterns of fight, flight, freeze, or faint to put you into survival mode. When we are in survival mode, we create unconscious, unwanted outcomes and results.

Only You Know Your Experience and What You Are Feeling

Discerning the five core emotions is where you begin to learn how to directly experience feelings. Numerous other terms such as frustrated, stressed, annoyed, insecure, and anxious, all are one, or a combination of the five core emotions. Anxiety is typically fear. Frustration and annoyance are often caused by anger or sexual feelings. Stress is often a combination of fear and anger. Know what you are feeling and become a master of knowing and being in your experience. It is helpful to break emotions down into the core feelings and identify what they are for you so you may know what *you* are experiencing—no one else.

When clients are invited to welcome their emotions, and allow energy to move freely, they feel more present. Such feelings were summed up by one of my clients: "I waste time and energy managing my feelings. Wow!"

Go Beyond Emotions

To become a master is to fully accept that emotions are *no big deal*. They are normal. The nervous system enables us to navigate through experiences; like waves at a beach, they come and go. Some waves are big. Some are small. Instead of riding the waves like a masterful surfer, we sit on the beach and *talk* about the waves. We judge them, rank them, observe them, getting lost in our thoughts. Should we walk around announcing every single emotion we are feeling? No! There are times when it is necessary and useful to repress emotions, but emotional energy is natural and continually repressing the energy is unhealthy. Breathing and moving support the nervous system in processing the life force energy necessary to sustain us as human beings. Wisdom and pure intelligence flow organically when we drop stories about emotions. When emotionally fluent, you will expand your vitality and strengthen your resilience.

Emotional Intelligence—Apply the Practice

Step 1: Notice the sensation in your body.

Step 2: Translate it to the appropriate feeling.

Step 3: Capture the wisdom and express it professionally and respectfully.

Step 4: Breathe and move to support your nervous system.

CREDIT ——————————————————

1 https://www.merriam-webster.com/dictionary/vulnerable

2 https://www.merriam-webster.com/dictionary/empathy

CHAPTER 6

STOP SURVIVING AND START EVOLVING

Emotional Intelligence 5.0

The main function of fear is to act as an alarm to danger, a threat, or motivational conflict, which then initiates unconscious natural adaptive responses that are a part of human evolution. Fear responses have evolved to protect us. These responses are very useful and necessary.

Avid hikers love being in nature. When in the forest, should a bear come along, it wouldn't be safe to sit and analyze solutions for a potential interaction with it. Contemplation such as these are dangerous. *Okay, I see a bear. It is coming to attack me. Hmm. What should I do? Should I run? Or should I stay? Should I fight the bear?* Survival is at stake. The brain and nervous systems are hard-wired for natural protective responses, but these responses are not helpful nor useful in everyday life.

There are reasons to feel scared or afraid in the workplace. These situations are not life-threatening, and survival is not at stake, but we need to consciously recognize the psychosomatic experience of them and pay attention when we act out or shut down and go into one or more of our conditioned fear responses: flight, fight, freeze, or faint.

The brain and nervous system are hard-wired for natural protective responses. These responses show up not only when we see a bear in the woods, but also where we don't need them. There is no level of better or worse response here. All are equally ineffective.

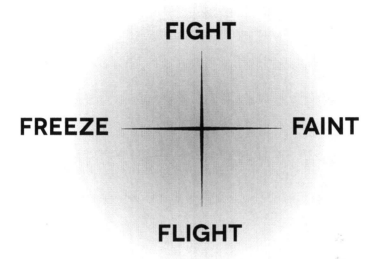

Figure 3

Fight Response

If a bear comes along while you're in the woods, the nervous system will automatically take over and may naturally fight him, such as picking up a stick and starting to hit him.

What the fight response looks like in the workplace is defensiveness. Symptoms include verbal and non-verbal defensiveness or attacks and repetitive explanations, reasons, and justification. The chin is forward, and the hands are acting out. Every verbal and non-verbal cue is that of a fighter boxing in the ring with no opponent, more vocal and noisy.

Flight Response

Taking flight or fleeing causes us to turn and run from the bear. At work, this may look like mentally tuning out during a meeting or looking at your laptop or phone. The body is there, but mentally, you've left the meeting, stopped participating, and are no longer present. Sometimes, people may *literally* walk out. Situations in high-growth companies where people become afraid that the culture is dying are only one example. They flee to another company and become scared when experiencing more change than they can handle, so they leave the team or company.

Freeze Response

With some bears, the appropriate response may be to freeze, become still, and hope the bear walks away. Deer freeze (*deer in the headlights*) at oncoming cars when they are frightened. When that happens to a person, going into mental and physical lock-down, so frightened or surprised you are frozen while at work that is a freeze response. This happens because you are scared; you usually aren't speaking, as if someone is waving a hand in front of your eyes, saying, "Hello? Is anyone home?"

At a coaching session with a technology engineer who had just moved from an Individual Contributor role into a manager role, he confessed he felt he wasn't making any progress as a manager. While reviewing his fear patterns, he realized he was scared of being a new manager and was *frozen* in his Individual Contributor tasks and functions. Once he realized this, he was able to move into action and perform his duties.

Faint Response

Part of the emotional response of fear at the bear in the woods is a drop in blood pressure. This sudden drop may cause you to faint, sending the message to the bear that you're already dead. In fact, with some bears, an appropriate response is to play dead.

In the workforce, this may look like *spacing out*. Clients describe their faint experience as, "I can't find the words," or "I go stupid," or "My thoughts become foggy, and I can't articulate what I want to say." Fainting is a self-protective strategy from too much stress on the nervous system.

Know Your Response with Compassion

Fear response patterns show up as a part of human instinct. Responses depend on the situation. When you're not present with yourself and feel scared, you may freeze or faint. When you freeze, you may be very still and may stop breathing and speaking. Recognize the symptoms of the secondary response—the faint response. You may not know what to say, and your sentences might be choppy and unclear. Recognize both responses. When I deliver keynote speeches, and the topic is emotional intelligence or presence, I point out *if* or *when* I freeze or faint. I rarely experience a flight response because I stick around. I don't leave. The fight response comes when someone tries to harm a friend of mine or when there has been some social injustice. That's when to become the fighting, angry activist.

All four responses are very useful when in danger. They are *not* useful when trying to work alongside or connect with others. Bring compassion by recognizing your responses and navigating your experience gracefully.

Stop Surviving and Start Evolving

Most people are in survival mode all the time and don't even realize it. The human body is an organism whose *primary* function and purpose are to survive, scanning the environment for what's wrong—the strong negativity bias in the world. We categorize people as friend or foe. Most of us have food, clothing, and shelter. We do not have to fight for basic needs. Despite this, we are still in survival mode. This is our opportunity to evolve beyond fear and simple survival.

The Physiology of Fear

When someone is in a fear response, it's like talking to a wall or a caged animal. You can't rationalize the irrational; they *will* act irrationally. Fear is the enemy of reason. The individual is not connected to themselves and has been hijacked by instinct. Because fear responses happen automatically and unconsciously, they don't realize they've been hijacked. Fear does not discriminate. We can see irrational behavior from CEOs, Ph.D.s, therapists, top-notch engineers, and presidents of anything.

There is a massive neurological and physiological—*and very real*—event that occurs in the body when in fear. The sympathetic nervous system engages. Part of the brain, the amygdala, processes sensory signals and generates a fear response by stimulating autonomic responses such as increased heart rate, increased blood pressure, and involuntary muscle reaction. Blood rushes to the core to protect the organs. During this response, the amygdala hi-jacks the prefrontal cortex, leading to narrowing of sight. This wipes out the ability to think clearly and intelligently.

People differ from animals regarding physiological events. A gazelle on the savanna won't engage the sympathetic nervous system unless there a is direct threat—a lion. It will try to outrun it and will need its sympathetic nervous system to do so. One of two things will happen: it will either outrun the lion or it won't. If it does, it's body knows to turn off its sympathetic nervous system and return to physiological homeostasis. Where humans differ is our sympathetic nervous system will engage when merely *thinking* about a threat. Even with no real threat, we go into survival mode based on thoughts of what might happen. To reiterate, this is a *real* physiological event. Physiology is fighting you. To make matters worse, there is no real threat, so your nervous system doesn't have an outlet to move the energy naturally—therefore we feel terrible, contracted, constricted, and uncomfortable, unable to think clearly. This exacerbates the experience and puts us into deeper survival mode.

We experience survival mode based on an infinite number of thoughts, and we create an experience centered around the belief that we are not psychologically safe.

- "If I don't do well, I won't get promoted."
- "If the project doesn't go well, will I lose my job?"
- "If I tell her the truth, I will hurt her feelings."
- "What will people think if I say I don't know?"
- "If I compare myself to others, I'm not good enough."
- "I should do better."
- "What will people think if I leave the company to align with my values?"
- "Last time I screwed it up. I better not do that again!"

Fear unconsciously runs most of our society. Many interlocking aspects of society have become increasingly sophisticated in communicating messages and information that produce fear responses. Advertising, political ads, news coverage, and social media all send the constant message that people should be afraid—very afraid. Because thoughts are so pervasive, fear is pervasive. We live in a culture of fear. Most people are in survival mode. We end up fearing the wrong things, incredibly out of proportion to reality. We have a much higher chance of being killed by lightning than by a terrorist.

A huge opportunity to evolve past survival mode is possible. Recognize your fear pattern and shift out of it by breathing through, and being with, the energy, and from there, pay attention to whatever wants attention. If you are simply following your thoughts, *stop!* Exhale to engage your parasympathetic nervous system. Breathe, move to support yourself, and come back to presence. Then ask, "What wants to happen now?" Most of all, gain insight from the experience of being in survival mode versus not. What caused you to be triggered? What worked for you to shift from survival mode? Time to raise your awareness.

Applying the Practice: Stop Surviving—Start Evolving

Step 1: Notice your fear pattern when you are in survival mode and stop!

Step 2: Exhale to turn off your sympathetic nervous system and engage your parasympathetic nervous system.

Step 3: Ask, "What can I pay attention to here or am I just following a thought?"

Step 4: Breathe and move to support your nervous system.

Step 4: Ask, "Now that I'm present, what wants to happen? What's here for me to learn?"

CHAPTER 7

PRESENCING—BE IN YOUR
DIRECT EXPERIENCE

Presence is being with what is, exactly as it is, directly, clearly and fully inhabiting our experience. If we do this, we are aligned with reality, and the truth of who we are comes through.

Presencing is the activity of *being* present. Runners run, artists paint, engineers code and conscious people *presence*. Presence is an action verb since it is the *process* of being present—the action and behavior of being with what *is*, just as it is, without trying to make anything different; meeting fully whatever is here and directly experiencing the same. You can't meet what is here and respond appropriately if you are not able to inhabit your experience. This may sound obvious and simple, but it isn't. Typically, we avoid our experience. There are many reasons. This practice is especially useful in intense situations.

- When we experience triggers and have been hijacked by fear
- When we feel a huge wave of emotion that intimidates us
- When we're constricted and don't understand why
- When we are resisting, feeling blocked, or stuck
- When we can't explain our experience and wonder, "What the heck is going on?

We avoid these uncomfortable experiences. Presencing is a way to *welcome* the experience. This compassionate and easeful state can be achieved while going about our day-to-day activities. Presencing opens awareness within and creates space for us to see beyond our surface activities, to capture any insights. Insight follows direct experience. When we are directly inhabiting our experience, we can tap into pure intelligence and the wisdom that is all around us.

Use the following practice anywhere: during a meeting, while you are walking, in a one-on-one with someone, or while you are alone. Each wave of energy will pass and move on when it's ready. By not denying your state of being, you will be able to capture insights into the timing of when they want to come forward.

Once you become skillful, you can presence anything in a matter of moments, and with mastery, inhabit your experience, so you no longer recognize it as an activity. Taking it slow is a powerful way to start. The practice of presencing will help you cultivate love and compassion in yourself and for others.

Applying the Practice: Presencing—Be in Your Direct Experience

> **Step 1**: Take a few easy breaths; continue easy breaths during the process.
>
> **Step 2**: Get comfortable.
>
> **Step 3**: Notice any sensations in your body. Feel your body against the floor, chair, or feel your feet on the ground. Continue to breathe.
>
> **Step 4**: Notice any emotions that are present—anger, joy, sadness, sexual feelings, fear.
>
> **Step 5**: Notice where, or what, you are resisting. Pay attention to any thoughts that arise, and let them pass on; do not add to them.

Step 6: Gently welcome and open to all that is here at the moment, as if welcoming a friend through your front door.

Step 7: Give your sensations, energy, emotions, everything, space to be here with you. Imagine allowing whatever is here to be here, without trying to change it, fix it, or make it go away. Breathe and be with it.

Step 8: Allow yourself to welcome what is here with gentleness, compassion, and love—no matter what is here—including any resistance or judgments. Do not get involved with what's here. Do not try to sort out thoughts. Let go of tendencies to problem-solve or try to figure it out. Allow for any stillness or silence without stirring.

Step 9: Listen to anything deeper, any wisdom under the surface of any sensations and emotions. Be prepared that insight may or may not come right away, and all that there is to do is to allow life force energy to flow through you organically.

CHAPTER 8

CONSCIOUS COMMITMENTS

The process and practice of conscious commitment is a direct path to wake up, evolve, and achieve the results you want in life and business. We are always committed to something, whether we are consciously or unconsciously aware of it. When we are consciously committed, we gather all our faculties and focus them in a chosen direction to produce the results we desire. We are awake to our actions. When we are asleep at the wheel, our unconscious choices affect our outcomes. To easily see what your current commitments are, look at results. Ask yourself, "What do I want normalized in my company? A conscious or unconscious culture?"

Commitment

A commitment is a pact with the universe. At the core, you're saying, "I am gathering my energy, all my faculties, thoughts, processes, time, money, relationships, and momentum toward a given direction. I am committed to being drama free." But, if you experience drama on your team, you are committed to drama. Results prove this regardless of what you claim. If you have the unconscious commitment to disrupting the project, you will find errors in it. If you are ineffective in your communications, and if they are not clear, you are committed to

CONSCIOUS COMMITMENTS | 63

unclear communications. The results show the current commitment regardless of what we say we want.

The old mentality, "Work hard and play hard," shows that if you are committed to life and work being hard, they *will* be hard. I was committed to *everything* being hard, so when things were easy, I made up the story that I wasn't being challenged. As soon as I committed that everything could be easy, everything *became* easy. Don't confuse easy with lazy. There is nothing lazy about stepping into a life of ease.

Work being hard is an old paradigm: *If you are not working hard, you must be goofing off. You must look busy, work hard, and push yourself. Experiences can be intense, challenging, and difficult to navigate.* By committing to ease, you won't affect the experience; you will affect how you *relate* to the experience.

The Neurology of Habits and Commitments

It's important to know the neurology of habits. Our unconscious commitments—our habits—get hardwired into a part of our brain, the basal ganglia, which stores routine habits and patterns. The reason for this is that our brains can be very efficient. We need to be as familiar as possible with all the nuances of our commitments to create new habits. It is *crucial* to be patient with ourselves and others. Patterns and habits are ingrained and neurologically wired, so we may find it difficult to move into the new commitment or habit right away. It may take time and energy to rewire them. Be compassionate with yourself and others. We all have our own patterns running, and we are all in this together.

We don't get what we want; we get what we are *committed* to. The process to unravel old patterns, step into conscious commitments, and evolve gracefully is demonstrated in Figure 4.

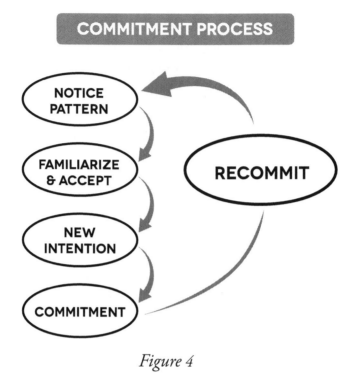

Figure 4

Four Steps to Unravel Conditioning and Create Conscious Commitments

Notice the pattern. To change an unconscious commitment to a conscious one, the first step is to notice and become aware of a pattern or conditioning. A pattern cannot be changed until it is recognized. Name it, and you will allow emotions to flow. Say, "Okay, I see a pattern and am not happy about the results—but I can face it!" Celebrate that you *notice* the pattern. When you do, you can create conditions to make a different choice. This is reason to celebrate.

Familiarize and accept. Step two is to familiarize and accept the pattern. Learn as much as possible about it and what triggers you. How does your mind strategize to keep the pattern going? Your brain is wired to maintain it, scanning the landscape, looking for evidence of what it expects. Become familiar with noticing what is triggering it.

Your mind will strategize and create conditions to keep your pattern in place by actively seeking out information to support its claim. Notice how you create conditions to keep it running. Notice what actions and situations you create to stay in the same loop of behavior. Self-acceptance is essential; accept the pattern you have running and how you create it.

> *The person who accepts himself,*
> *whatever his real or imagined shortcomings*
> *can move from self-awareness*
> *to the attainment of new understanding*
> *and new integrations,*
> *to the attainment of a superior manner*
> *of being and of functioning.*
>
> – NATHANIEL BRANDEN

During this phase, you may be entertained by your abilities to keep the strategy—the pattern—in place. Your mind will strategize beyond all sorts of belief. Consider the energy your nervous system requires doing that; that's energy you could use for something more productive. This is where you free up life force energy. If you are beating yourself up about what you see in *you*, you create resistance and tension and hold the pattern in place. Resistance creates exhaustion, drains energy, and decreases your level of vitality. The shift takes place when you hold yourself lightly.

New intention. Having familiarized yourself and accepted your pattern, begin to think about new choices. "What do I *really* want?" Begin to act toward it. Setting a new intention is an experimental phase where you play with what you want, and notice what's in alignment with who you are and how you appear to the world.

Commitment. You will experience a noticeable difference as you become ready to make a pact with the universe. You will have the feeling,

"I am ready to make a new choice and shift into a new commitment," or "I am ready to take all my energy, faculties, thoughts, feelings, and actions toward a chosen direction." You may even say it out loud, "I commit to . . .."

Recommit After Falling Back into the Old Behavior

"What happens if I make this new commitment and go back to my old pattern?" Once you've created a new commitment, at times you will drift back into the old pattern of the neurologically-wired habit, especially when stressed. If that happens, say, "Okay, there I go. I drifted to the old pattern. I recommit." It's that simple. You may drift back into the old behavior a few times or even a few hundred times. Gather yourself and recommit. The point is, you are in the driver's seat. You may have taken a wrong turn again, but what do you do? Turn around and get back on the right road.

Step into Commitments

Examples of Core Commitments:
- I commit to mastery of the practice of presence.
- I commit to my primary marriage to the truth.
- I commit to taking responsibility for my actions.
- I commit to presencing my emotions as a way of being.
- I commit to a life of gratitude.
- I commit to a life of ease.
- I commit to a life of conscious communication free of gossip.
- I commit to prioritizing connection and intimacy over being right and over perpetuating my conditioned patterns.
- I commit to a highly conscious, fully present, relationship with technology. I commit to using technology to support my purpose, values, and vitality.

- I commit to seeing every moment as an opportunity to learn, grow, and evolve.

- I commit to learning all I can about my unconscious bias, stereotyping, and how I exclude others.

- I commit to being a producer on the planet versus a consumer and being a responsible steward of the planet's resources.

- I commit to high self-esteem and to supporting others in high self-esteem.

Use this list as a starting point, and your determine commitments in the language that resonates with you. It is the most effective way to wake up from the trance and evolve.

Applying the Practice: Consciously Commit and Recommit

Step 1: Notice the pattern.

Step 2: Familiarize yourself with it and accept it.

Step 3: Experiment with a new intention.

Step 4: Step into a conscious commitment.

Step 5: Recommit if you fall back into the old behavior.

CHAPTER 9

CONSCIOUS EXPRESSION

Responding to Life

This chapter addresses how to speak, how to express yourself consciously, and how you respond verbally and nonverbally. People struggle the most in relating to others. Their inner experience does not match their outer expression and therefore, getting along with others becomes difficult, especially regarding communication. This is an opportunity to evolve with great acceleration. For when are truly real with each other, then we can connect on a deeper level.

The goal here is awareness, not perfection. The goal is to close the gap between your inner experience and how you appear. When the inner experience of someone matches their outer expression, the truth comes forward. Strength of mind and character, and a level of maturity that goes beyond anything we've seen so far, especially in our relationships, is what is required to respond to life with ability and responsibility. With conscious expression, lazy and sloppy conversations and interactions can be minimized, making for richer connection.

Why Is It So Difficult to Communicate?

When we drift from presence, we deny the truth of who we are. Expressions are loaded with content and small talk because we are avoiding the pain of the current moment. We deny truth and reality. These example depict the widest gap between appearance and truth:

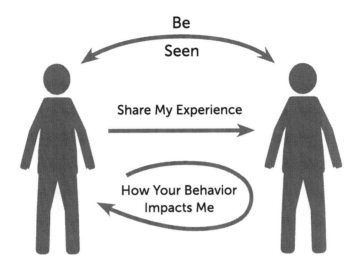

Figure 5

- We are addicted to drama and communicate from a persona.
- We converse through blaming, shaming, whining, and complaining.
- We fill the space between us with platitudes.
- We are triggered and react defensively.
- We gossip because we're not willing to state what's true for us.
- We cover up feelings with anything but the truth and end up speaking incongruently.
- We don't know how to consciously express our feelings, especially anger, so we attack.
- We make up the story that we will offend someone else with what we say.
- We are not present and in our experience, so we express from mind chatter rather than dropping into our inner wisdom. Insight follows experience, as will an appropriate response.
- Our fear pattern hijacks our brain, so we don't think clearly and don't express ourselves clearly.

- We become intimidated by the life force energy flowing in our nervous system, and we try to move it with a lot of words, reporting rather than connecting. Some of us love to hear ourselves talk.

- We fall into the trap of low self-esteem, or Imposter Syndrome, with thoughts like, "I'm not good enough." As a result, we don't speak at all, or what we do say is so managed, it's awkward.

- We aren't aware of various aspects of our style differences and aren't able to exercise our communication muscles.

- We take our attention from ourselves and direct it toward others, instead of paying attention to our own communication.

- We aren't clear in what we want or don't want and don't make clear requests.

It's all about conditioning and unconscious behavior. These examples demonstrate how we run on autopilot. Instead of genuinely tuning into how we want to consciously connect and appropriately respond, we drift from presence and rely on conditioned patterns for what comes out of our mouths. Conditioning is useful to help us get things done, but not useful when connecting with others. Human interactions are very fluid. We must be able to respond appropriately in the moment, to respond with ability and responsibility.

Watch out for projections. We deny parts of ourselves and ascribe them to others. This becomes the predominant behavior from which we communicate. Webster defines projection as *"the attribution of one's own attitudes, feelings, suppositions, or desires to someone or something as a naive or unconscious defense against anxiety or guilt."* [1] Through projections, we communicate *you* statements directed at others but intended for us.

This denial and transference to another as a defense mechanism is common. We have blind spots, and it's hard for us to see our own failings. But it can be easy for us to see what's wrong with other people, particularly work colleagues and spouses. We are mirrors for each other and see clearly what we don't like, but we get it backwards. It's not them;

it's us. We want to believe what we want to believe, so we feel safe by ascribing the behavior to someone else. Furthermore, by disowning any part of our self, our self-esteem immediately takes a hit for the worse.

Blaming and shaming are classic examples of projections we use to avoid discomfort. Undesirable thoughts, motivations, desires, emotions, compartmentalizations, and excitations that split outside our ego are perceived in others. This action maintains a self-created illusion. These strategies are ways our ego maintains the illusion that we are completely in control. While engaged in such behavior, we are unable to access truthful memories, intentions, and experiences, even about our own nature.

Projections directly break any connection with us and others. For impactful conversations, projecting back and forth is a waste of time and energy. The ability to discern when we are projecting creates opportunities to evolve.

Some Real-life Examples

- The individual who accuses their spouse of wanting to have an affair when it is they having an affair

- The executive coach who tells the client, "You have issues with authority," when it is the client who struggles with authority figures

- "You don't listen"—a client's remark to a colleague in defense of something said to him when it was he who wasn't listening

- "Your feedback is too subjective"—a manager's very subjective comment in an email to a client

- The individual who claims her family is judgmental and doesn't know how to connect, when it is she who judges everyone and doesn't know how to create satisfying interactions

- Parents who project all their hopes, dreams, and values onto their children without checking in with them, what they want, and what their values are

- The workshop participant who tells a third party the facilitator was bored during class, when it was he who was bored and didn't speak up; this individual told the facilitator that he was "checking the box" at the beginning of the workshop

- The businessman who claims his partner is untrustworthy, when it was he who didn't keep in alignment with a contractual agreement and refused to pay his share of the capital required in the formal, legal, signed contract

- The executive who raves about everyone else, when is he who avoids his own discomfort with being successful, projecting positive qualities as much as negative ones

Many people are a mystery to themselves and are virtually sleepwalking. They project by taking attributes from others unconsciously and ascribing them to themselves or back onto others. I call this the pinball effect. You may be saying, *"I never do that."* Examine yourself. You may notice that you are making *you* statements. Ask yourself, *"Am I projecting to avoid something uncomfortable in myself?"* Instead of projecting, stop yourself, take responsibility, and share your experience with the intention to evolve.

Why is Conscious Expression so Important?

Knowledge, wisdom and connection are the commodities in an information age. The ability to behave effectively together is a core skill. We collaborate to get things done and impact the world, and how we relate is as important as the product we sell. "If awareness never reaches beyond superficial events and current circumstances, actions will be reactions. If, on the other hand, we penetrate more deeply to see the larger whole that generates what is and our own connection to this wholeness, the source and effectiveness of our actions can change dramatically."[2]

It's time to shift from survival mode and begin to evolve alongside others. Communicating for connection, growth, and learning is a more fulfilling experience. The underlying goal of all these practices is to be connected and bring us closer. Nowhere is that more relevant than how we respond in the moment. Human interactions are fluid. We cannot treat each other like robots. While there is no formula for connecting, structure allows us to organize our thoughts when responding. Here's the *how*—an un-formula.

How to Respond to Life and Speak Consciously

To be able to respond consciously and congruently, our outer expression must match our inner experience. In aligning, a natural feedback loop is created with others that includes two elements.

Truth: My experience of *me* while I am interacting with *you*.

Non-Truth: My experience of *you* while interacting with *me*.

Presence is the foundation for everything. This organic feedback loop invites us to stay present, connected to ourselves, and connected to others. By sharing *me* while interacting with *you*, *you* get a chance to know and see *me*, and I bring *myself* closer to *me*. Only I know the truth of my experience, and I can't know me unless I am sharing my experience—what's true for me. This includes *I* statements and facts. The truth includes body sensations, feelings, thoughts, reactions, uncertainties, requests, and boundaries, expressed with a clear *yes* or *no*.

One of the most profound parts of our experiences and motivations is our feelings, and we are given virtually *no* education in how to deal with them. Emotional intelligence is required to respond appropriately. If we aren't present, and if we aren't present with our emotions, we won't speak from a place of genuine experience.

Clearly, facts are important when expressing, therefore they must be included in communication. A fact has actual existence, something measurable and observable. Facts equal emotions that we feel. They do not equal emotions we *think* we are feeling—that's a thought.

By sharing the experience of *you* while interacting with *me*, I share how *you* are coming across to *me* and the impact of your communication and behavior on me. By sharing *my* experience of *you*, an open dialog is created where *we* get to know each other, *see* each other, and evolve together.

Only we know the truth of our experience; others can only guess. When sharing non-truthful statements such as opinions, stories, intuitions, awareness, even judgments, we are sharing any facts that we observe and *you* statements. The impact of others' behavior on us includes stories, judgments, opinions, intuitions, estimations of emotions, and anything else about the experience.

There is an argument here that I hear many times: *"But I'm sure I know what's going on with them, so what am I seeing in them is the truth."* We don't operate in an interpersonal vacuum. While we will have some idea of what is happening for the other person, we cannot truly know their inner experience. We shut down connection and dialogue as soon as we are married to our idea of what the other person is thinking, feeling, etc. Check this out for yourself; only you know what's true for you. Consider which the following statements are more evolved:

This: "You are such an idiot. You keep cutting me off!"

Or: "I notice I feel angry, and I'm losing my ability to stay present and connected with you. I don't want to share my ideas (my experience of me). You are coming across as very dismissive (my experience of you). We've been in this meeting for forty minutes, and you've interrupted me four times (facts). Would you be willing to hear me out?

Here is another example:

This: "You are a jerk."

Or: "I feel like attacking you."

Notice in this exchange the subtle, but substantial, difference. Sharing the truth that you are triggered and want to attack someone is very different than *actually* attacking them.

Research shows that the brain contextualizes everything. Memories really aren't accurate therefore we must let go the idea that we know exactly what another person is experiencing or what they did. There's much more to say about the advances in science that is not investigated here. People don't speak "fact to fact", therefore we must be more conscious.

Applying the Practice: Conscious Expression—Responding to Life

Step 1: Make sure you are breathing. To be masterful at communicating, this is the first step. The brain uses 20 percent of the body's oxygen supply, three times more than the muscles. With these statistics, you must become an expert at breathing into your belly to be an effective connector. Exhale, inhale, then speak.

Step 2: Notice when you are present or not present. Mastery of presence is mastery of connection. You can't share your experience unless you are in your experience. When you are present, you should respond in the moment rather than communicating from a persona. Stop your mind chatter and get present—silence first, then speak. "Real communication can take place only where there is silence."3 Breathe, then speak.

Step 3: Share my experience of me while interacting with you or others. Match your inner experience with your external expression—be congruent. Be seen. Share all aspects of your experience. You can't be connected to another person if you are not connected to yourself; breathing, present, and being in the truth of your experience will create inner connection.

Step 4: Share my experience of you or others while interacting with me. Share with the other person how they came across to you, what you are noticing, and what may be familiar to you. This is where you can invite them to come closer. Accept that you cannot know someone else's experience until they let you see them.

Step 5: Create space for others to receive what you are saying. Once you have shared, stop talking and listen. Give the receiver a chance to accept your words and take them in. A word or two inviting them to respond may be called for here.

Step 6: Stay in your current experience. As the conversation continues, keep breathing and notice if you are present; then allow the loop to continue. Be aware of your tone, cadence, and pacing. Here the dialogue can continue. You may have a specific request, or perhaps the dialogue wants to stop.

Which Dialogue is More Evolved?

This: "You always trying to control everything!"

Or: "I feel tired when interacting with you at meetings. I must put in far more effort than I want. At the last five team meetings, you appeared to be pushing your own agenda rather than what's best for the group. I heard you say, 'We must do it this way.' I feel impacted in my ability to respect you. Can you tell me what's going on for you?"

This: "You don't know what you are talking about!"

Or: "I feel really rattled. You remind me of my spouse, constantly pointing out what I'm doing wrong. I feel like I want to villainize you. I'm wondering if you'd give me a minute to gather myself."

This: "It's your fault the project has stalled, not mine."

Or: "I feel angry. We agreed that we would meet the deadline by today. I've completed my part. I hear you haven't finished your part. I'm starting to think you had no intention of participating. I have a lot of judgments about you right now. Would you be willing to explain what happened?"

This: "You are a racist."

Or: "When I read your post on Facebook, I felt scared and angry. I was shocked and didn't know how to respond. In fact, I feel afraid to bring this up. Your comments came across to me as racist, and I am deeply disturbed. I think it could negatively affect others. Would you be willing to share your thought process?"

When people are consciously communicating, this doesn't mean everyone agrees. Collaboration does not necessarily equal consensus. It does mean that everyone can express their side of any issue without blaming or shaming and without being blamed or shamed. We can agree to disagree. Although everyone may not agree on a course of action, we must be united. When we leave the room, it's important to not create drama by gossiping or badmouthing anyone.

Agree to a course of action, then act. Gather feedback and iterate. There's zero value in saying *"I told you so,"* or *"We should have done it my way."* A more mature response would be, *"I feel angry, and I feel strongly about my point of view. In the future, how can I express this in a way that's more effective, and in a way that is more compelling so that you listen? I would like to try to avoid this in the future as a lot of time was invested into this initiative, and we didn't make progress."*

Does it take more time and energy to express more consciously? Yes! And the short-term investment makes for noticeable returns going forward.

Conscious Expression—See Others and Be Seen

When we see others and are seen, we discover the potential in every moment while working alongside colleagues. We connect and feel safe. The requirement is to reveal the truth of who you are instead of withholding. When we withhold our experience, we are not present, and we're going against an organic and fresh response. We no longer need to keep secrets. Conscious expression allows us to respect our personal privacy by saying, *"I would rather not reveal that right now. I would prefer to keep that private and not dilute my experience."*

By aligning your outer expression with your inner experience, you build internal trust that what comes out of your mouth includes compassion. There is safety in trusting yourself. When you trust yourself, trusting others isn't necessary. There are no more elephants in the room. With the skill to communicate, you can say anything to anyone, and the time between recognizing a problem and talking about it disappears.

Conscious expression invites you to move away from blaming, shaming, gossiping, dramatizing, projecting, politicking, and other reactive behaviors because a container of respect is created before you react, correct, or inspect any situation. A culture of responsibility—self-accountability, as well as overall accountability—is the result of communicating clearly from a place of presence.

Another reason expressing yourself consciously is so important is efficiency of time. Hours are wasted when we argue, try to explain ourselves, and engage in dialogue where no one is connected. It's a lot more fun to work in an environment where creative ideas are welcome, no matter how far-fetched. Conscious communication opens the door to innovation and connection. Wouldn't you rather be in a culture of people who communicate with transparency and presence, versus ego and drama?

Final Thoughts

You are probably thinking, *"What if the other person is not speaking consciously? What if they are attacking me or being disrespectful?"* This *will* happen—guaranteed. The only thing you can control in any situation is *you*. Focus on how you are showing up. Even if the conversation ends poorly, you want to be able to say, *"I was present, clear, and compassionate. I did all I could to create conditions for us to connect."*

Be compassionate as you and others are learning how to express yourselves. Throughout the process of learning this, you will see the ways you are on autopilot when you're speaking. Patterns will start to emerge. The more you see these patterns, the more you can consciously choose how you show up and connect with others.

Commit to being a master of conscious expression. The easiest way to cultivate a real conversation with others is to start with you. Make the commitment to lead by revealing your experience, if for no other reason than it's the type of leader and person you want to be and because of the impact you will have in the world.

In all interactions, make your primary goal being connected to the other person, rather than being right. With a genuine desire to be closer to others, you will notice a remarkable difference in your ability to speak effectively.

Finally, all of this is simple, but not easy. Initially staying on auto-pilot feels easier; however, it is not sustainable. Just like all of the skills being taught in this book, being a conscious and awakened human being or leader is not for the faint of heart. If you're comprehending these skills and are interested, you are up for the challenges and willing to overcome conditioning. Wake up and experience peace and freedom. Applaud yourself for the desire to evolve.

CREDIT ——————————————————

1 http://www.dictionary.com/browse/projection

2, 3 Senge, P., & Scharmer, C., & Jaworski J., 7 Flowers, B. (2004). Presence: Human Purpose and the Field of the Future. New York: Random House, Inc.

CHAPTER 10

MASTERFUL LISTENING

Consciously listening is a way to give attention to others. Leaders can show care by being masterful listeners. It can change the way you are perceived and how you connect with others. It speeds up the productivity of everyone involved in a project. It is also one of the most desired leadership traits by employees.

Everyone wants to be listened to and heard. Listening keeps us connected. Take a moment and reflect on how it feels when someone is listening. We feel acknowledged, understood, and heard. When others are actively paying attention to what we're saying, we immediately feel more connected because we have been heard and validated. By keeping our connection with others, we are more inclined to be real in conversations. We close off new ways of thinking when we are not listening. When we feel that our insights are acknowledged, we are more likely to present our original ideas, knowing that the other person will appreciate our input.

Listening also brings efficiency to communication in our day-to-day interactions. By listening, we get to the point of what is important to the other person so that any issue can be moved forward quickly and efficiently.

What Keeps Us from Listening?

Here are a few things that hinder our ability to listen effectively.

- We have an agenda that we want to get to. We stop hearing others so we can jump to the topic that is consuming us, thinking we are saving time when we are wasting it.

- We are distracted with something else and aren't available to the other person, whether we want to be or not. We may have just left a meeting that was intense, and issues were unresolved, and we aren't present to ourselves. If we aren't present, we won't be able to listen.

- We are mentally and physically drained. We have compassion and care about others and want to listen, but we are too tired. Consequently, we override our exhaustion, try to participate in the conversation, and end up drifting from presence.

- We aren't in the present moment. When we aren't present, we aren't listening.

- We are lazy or sloppy. Listening requires active engagement and real energy. It is also a skill that must be practiced and, just like everything else, when we don't practice, we are sloppy.

- Allowing ourselves to be hijacked by our thoughts, we confuse what is said with what we think is said. In short, we make up a story about what we think we heard versus listening to what was said. For instance, someone may be speaking about a situation they are experiencing with a colleague. Rather than paying attention, we think they want our advice about the circumstance. We start providing suggestions on how to remedy the matter.

Most of us have an unconscious listening filter that we use to attempt to expedite conversations, and by using this filter, we add static to our communication. We aren't listening so we are counterproductive, lose connection with others, and block innovation by making assumptions. Some common listening filters are to fix, control, or confirm a point of view, seek approval, avoid conflict, be right, or hear if we are liked. A classic interchange between two people is racing for the victim persona.

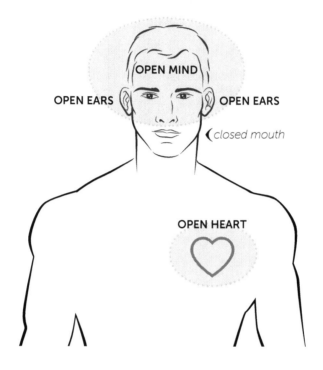

Figure 6

Two or more people are listening to see who can be the bigger victim. To identify your primary listening filter, pay attention to what's happening to you when someone is speaking. You may be thinking of a response or something you want to say rather than listening until the other person is finished. Even conscious listening can be a filter. You may be practicing so hard to try to consciously listen that you aren't listening.

The importance of listening is reflected this. At a meeting with three C-suite executives from a high growth, very successful technology company where change is constant, as is a heavy workload. Each executive had a listening filter. One was listening to fix, and he kept presenting solutions prematurely. Another was listening to control by trying to direct the conversation to her topic. The third individual was listening to avoid conflict by offering positive comments to anything that was said. The group went off task. I revealed to them that I was drifting into my filter of listening to fix. They became curious and realized that they were doing the same by not listening to each other. We all smiled at our awareness and brought the conversation back on track. Instead of this meeting extending over the hour time frame allotted, we ended ten minutes early.

A colleague once said, "I don't want you to do anything; I just want you to listen." My response was, "Wow. Nothing to do here but listen." This was an amazing *ah-ha* moment for me. Now I realize the power of those words. You can take executive presence to the next level by listening and acknowledging the other person. Listening is one of the skills people struggle with most. When we are consciously listening, workflow is easy, and productivity increases exponentially.

A Masterful Listener

Drop your agenda and give your full attention to the person who is speaking for the sole purpose of listening to and hearing them. Get present; stop talking. Listen to them and take in their words. Make sure you are breathing. Let the words vibrate through you. Let your speaker's words land on you, and let them resonate in you. Try them on so that you really get a feel for what the speaker is saying and understand their words and feelings. Put yourself in their shoes.

Ask, "Do you want me to respond or just listen here?" or "What I heard you say is . . .." After the speaker is finished, you might say, "Do you feel heard?" Listening is as much about letting the other person's words vibrate through you as it is verbally acknowledging what they said.

A note on the speaking side of a conversation—as they are talking, take responsibility for your communication. Ask for what you want and make a simple request. "I just want you to listen to me, and I'm not seeking comments right now. I want to hear any information you have about this situation."

Conscious listening can be a challenging skill to master. As you practice, notice your improvements and monitor your progress. Ask friends and colleagues if they've noticed a difference.

Of all the leadership skills, listening is by far the one people experience as the most difficult. I challenge my clients to go through an hour in their day listening; doing nothing else but listening to others. They tell me how they struggle with being silent and listening to the others. By making conscious listening our primary goal—listening and hearing others—we enhance our relationships, becoming closer to people.

Applying the Practice: Masterful Listening

Step 1: Drop your agenda and focus on the other person.

Step 2: Let their words land on you. Try them on and let them vibrate through you.

Step 3: Ask them, "Do you want me to comment here or just listen?"

Step 4: Notice and celebrate your improvements.

CHAPTER 11

FEEDBACK 101

Feedback is one of the toughest interactions for people. Companies today state, "We are a culture of feedback." But they don't define what that is, and people aren't sure why it's so difficult to communicate.

What is feedback? It's important to make this distinction to know if what you want to convey is feedback. Websters.com defines it as "a reaction or response to a particular process or activity; evaluative information derived from such a reaction or response; knowledge of the results of any behavior as influencing or modifying further performance."[1]

Next, ask, "What's my relationship to feedback?" We all have a unique relationship to giving and receiving feedback. During facilitation, I ask my clients to describe this relationship. Here are just a few of the responses I have received. "It's negative," "It's a gift," "It's helpful," "It's okay if the intention is good." One client described feedback as "Here comes the hammer." He physically backed up in his chair, as if to protect himself, while discussing his relationship to receive feedback. Often people don't know how to effectively say what they want to convey, or they don't know how to deliver feedback respectfully.

This receiving of feedback is neither good nor bad. It's your perspective and how you react to it that makes it positive or negative. When applied consciously, feedback leads to greater collaboration, and the sharing of knowledge, wisdom, and technical information. It creates a fast path to development, higher levels of effectiveness, accelerated learning, and opens a path to innovation. Moment-to-moment feedback flows between individuals during everyday interactions.

Feedback can become sticky and unclear. Under most circumstances, we unconsciously disguise some other motive as feedback. A request can be disguised as feedback, such as "speak more softly" or "work faster." When expressed as "you're being loud," or "the project isn't going fast enough," you may notice the subjectivity. One person may think you're too loud, but another may think your tone is right on. Someone may not be happy with the pace of the project, while another person is enjoying it. Consider the individual who heard from others that a colleague was gossiping about her. She tried to give feedback to him and struggled. She requested that instead of gossiping about her, that he speak directly to her. Once they were clear about this, their conversations were very productive and brought them closer, strengthening their relationship. Making a direct request can influence the other person to do what we want by giving correct feedback.

Sometimes a projection may be disguised as feedback. Frequently we deny parts of ourselves and ascribe them to others and end up giving feedback to others intended for ourselves. We project any disowned part of us onto another. We deny some quality in our self, usually a negative one, and ascribe it to another. This is a defense mechanism. The projection of our unconscious qualities onto another is quite common.

Projections directly break any connection with you and the other person. By way of impactful conversations, projecting back and forth is a waste of time and energy. The ability to discern when we are projecting versus providing feedback will save time and energy. One client, projecting onto his colleague, said, "You don't listen." He responded, "Your feedback is too subjective." The colleague disowned the very behavior he ascribed to his colleague.

Many time we suppress our feelings—typically anger and fear—and give a *no* to how things are being handled. Rather than speaking up, we evaluate the situation and give negative feedback. When things haven't gone our way, we may become scared and evaluate the circumstance negatively. We take our repressed emotional energy and ascribe it to someone else.

Other times, we are triggered—consciously or unconsciously—by another person's behavior and then evaluate their behavior as bad. We say things like, "You are not a good culture fit," or "You weren't effective." We aren't examining the truth and are blaming or shaming someone else, disguising it as feedback.

When we aren't aware of our style differences, we criticize others for not *doing it right*. They may be presenting something in a style that we don't like and, instead of requesting additional information, give them negative feedback, or we unconsciously impose our own style onto them and only give positive feedback if they match our style.

We may be in a conversation where someone has gaps in skill level or needs specific instruction. We see an opportunity to transfer, share wisdom, suggest a solution—an opportunity to share expertise. This is a training or teaching discussion, not feedback. Showing someone an accepted process or procedure is not feedback; it's a teaching moment: showing someone how to code something, explaining an expense report process, or project management. A new employee might say, "I have some feedback for you. You aren't doing that right," sending the message that "You are bad." Instead, a more truthful statement would be, "We have a process for that. Would you like me to show you?"

Leaders sometimes disguise direct commands as feedback. While the old *command and control* style of leadership is extremely outdated and ineffective, even in the flattest of organizations, leaders need to give commands. It's okay to say, "I need it done this way," rather than "You're not doing it right and can improve."

See why feedback is confusing? Skillfully giving and receiving feedback will open the door to a clearer understanding of what you want to communicate. To maximize your productivity and effectiveness, it would benefit you to use a conscious process when giving and receiving feedback.

How to Receive Feedback

There are many reactions to receiving feedback. Some people ignore it and tune out. Some shut down, and some deflect the feedback with a defensive statement. Typically, everyone fears reactions. In all these situations, we lose connection with ourselves and others.

When receiving feedback, get present to what is being said or experienced. If someone is giving you feedback, pay attention to your posture. Are your arms crossed? Do you have a closed posture? Make eye contact with the individual to let them know you have their attention. Don't be afraid to say, "No thank you. I'm not available right now." If you are open to the feedback in the moment, listen to what they are saying. Get curious. Try on the feedback, and see if it applies to you. Appreciate the individual for the offering. Reflect on it. Ask yourself, "Have I been late for meetings? Could any of this be true?" If your answer is *yes,* this could be valuable information.

Perhaps you receive feedback, and you try it on, realizing the individual giving the feedback made a generalization from *one* situation. Check in with yourself; determine that being late was beyond your control, and there was nothing for you to do. Then thank the person for offering the feedback and move forward.

In all cases, respond. Avoid getting pulled into their demand that you change and transform on the spot, and respond. "Thank you" is usually the best.

- "Thank you for letting me know. I will consider that."
- "Thank you for sharing your thoughts with me. I want to think about it overnight."

- "Thank you, but that's a lot for me to take in right now, and I want to let you know I heard you."

- "Thank you for letting me know. As I try on what you are saying, it doesn't resonate. Would you be willing to provide some specific details?"

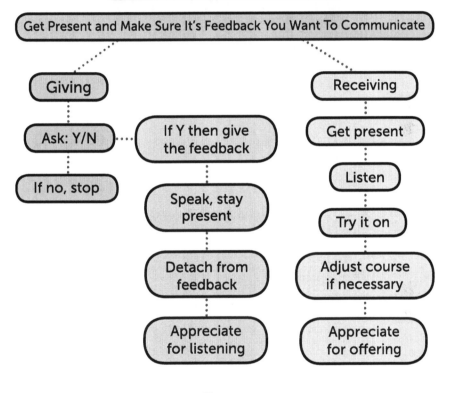

Figure 7

Notice in all these responses to start with *"Thank you."* With that, you are setting a tone of appreciation.

When receiving feedback, it is very important to pay attention to *what* is being said versus *how* it's being said. We react differently to incoming information depending on the tone in which it is delivered. Research shows we don't get upset about *what* people are saying to us, but *why* we think it's being said. By paying attention to the actual information, we bypass unnecessary and unproductive conversation, actions, and reactions. This cuts through drama and produces rapid results. You can always ask someone to deliver the message in a respectful tone, and then move on to the actual information. Being conscious of your relationship to receiving feedback enables you to discern any action items as a result of that feedback.

There is an organic, higher-level feedback loop that conscious and evolved humans know to give their attention. When receiving feedback from our environment and experiencing undesirable outcomes, the same applies—try it on. If the outcome of a project isn't what we want it to be, one reaction might be to think of it as a failure. However, if we choose to look at the outcome as feedback, we can adjust our course to get back on track. We might launch a product that is not showing success with consumers, or experience a software rollout that's not going smoothly. If we consciously use that information as inspiration to create new actions, we can get back on the path to a more desirable outcome.

On a personal level, if you find yourself dissatisfied in your interactions or you aren't meeting personal goals, this is a feedback loop. Pay attention to your environment so you can adjust your course as necessary. Conscious people will not conduct their personal or professional life in a fog. How we interact in all environments is a natural feedback loop.

Giving Feedback

To give feedback to another person, first check in with yourself, and see if it's necessary that you give evaluative information. Are you giving feedback when you really want something else, or is it for what you are projecting? Get present with yourself and ask, *"What is my motive?"* Is it *to move the issue forward, champion the person, or for creativity and information sharing?* If so, then proceed.

When giving feedback, ask the person for permission before you offer it. Specifically say, "Would you like feedback?" or "Would you like a suggestion?" or "Would you like some advice?" We waste enormous amounts of energy giving feedback when the individual isn't available or present. By asking first, we give them an opportunity to connect with us, get present, and determine if they are available. If the answer is *no*, don't give the feedback—and don't make up stories about their experience.

We create stories like, "He isn't open to feedback," or "She isn't interested in learning," or "He doesn't care what I think." These are all stories and invite drama. What may be true is that they have a meeting that starts in a couple of minutes and don't have time to listen fully to what you say. They may be immersed in a project and don't want to be distracted because a deadline is looming. They may want to hear your suggestion, but would rather hear it another time. Don't waste your time and energy making up a story about the other person. Just listen and wait for a more appropriate moment.

There are times you may want to insist. You may have some information about a project that you think is crucial for its success. Go ahead and say so. Tell them you think it's important and if it isn't said, the project may suffer. Remember, it is still their prerogative to say *yes* or *no*. If it's a *no*, do not give the feedback. This practice creates an environment of respect and trust.

If they answer *yes*, give the feedback. This is much more effective than saying to them, "You are dismissive."

Set the context: "At our last four teams meetings . . ."

Be specific: "You interrupted Raj, John, and Keisha while they were presenting their ideas."

Speak of impact: "I'm noticing a trend where they are no longer speaking up, and it's important that we hear diverse ideas so we can make a stronger impact."

Offering of connection: "Does any of this resonate? Can I provide some more specifics?"

Once you've delivered the feedback, stop talking and give them a chance to try it on, think about it, and ask follow-up questions. Many of us do the *dump and run*, where we give feedback and then walk away. Notice how you are giving the feedback. Are you delivering the information with the style of a floating feather, a jackhammer, or a cannonball at short range? Stay engaged with them, and be prepared to answer any questions and make space for their feelings and experience. Appreciate them for listening.

Detach from them acting on your feedback. This is the most difficult thing to do—to drop expectations that they will do anything with your feedback. We waste a lot of time and energy trying to change others, expecting them to transform right before our eyes. When we focus that time on ourselves and our own projects, we can direct our energy toward more productive causes. Harness your own time and energy by detaching from whether or not someone will act on your feedback.

Finally, when giving feedback, most people tend to focus on the things they want to see improved. Shift your mindset to also give feedback about what is going well. Use the same process and ask them first. When they are present, convey the positive information.

Notice how positive feedback is far more effective.

Set the context: "At the all hands meeting yesterday . . ."

Be specific: "You were clear in all your points. Your slides were very inviting. Your pacing and tone felt accurate."

Speak of impact: "I and others felt inspired by your message, and I feel encouraged to do more."

Offering of connection: *"Does any of this resonate? Can I provide some more specifics?"*

Facing mistakes is important and teaches us, but we can focus on what's going well and learn from that, too. Give feedback on what is going well. Blow people away by asking for permission and then conveying only positive news. Awaken and be an exceptional partner to humanity.

Applying the Practice: Receiving Feedback

Step 1: Hear the feedback, and try it on.

Step 2: Adjust your course, if necessary.

Step 3: Appreciate the individual for sharing their feedback with you.

Step 4: When receiving feedback from the environment on an undesired outcome, get curious. Ask, "What can I learn here? How can I course-correct?"

Applying the Practice: Giving Feedback

Step 1: Get present with yourself and ask, "Do I have some real feedback to convey?"

Step 2: Ask permission before giving feedback to someone. If the answer is yes, proceed with the feedback. If the answer is no, do not give the feedback.

Step 3: Be specific versus judgmental.

Step 4: Detach from the receiver doing anything about it.

Step 5: Appreciate the individual for listening.

CREDIT ————————————————

1 http://dictionary.reference.com/browse/feedback?s=t

CHAPTER 12

A CULTURE OF EVOLUTION

Seeking always to expand awareness—a commitment to learning—therefore, a commitment to growth as a way of life.

—NATHANIEL BRANDEN

This is an invitation to take a fresh and provocative viewpoint on feedback. Do you want people interacting all day by evaluating each other, knowing that most of the time we are not present, in survival mode, and projecting? No! *Most of what we call feedback does not need to be delivered.* The opportunity for accelerated growth, learning, and evolution is immense. Business provides the conditions for us to evolve as human beings—so rid yourself of the culture of feedback, and welcome a culture of evolution.

Contrary to how most people live, life is a journey, not a destination. For many of us, the path of that journey is through business. There is no other time in history where *how* we interact is as important as *what* we do. Be open to growth and learning as a way of life. The human species is being asked to evolve, sustaining a mindset of learning will allow us the ability to evolve gracefully.

Many leaders stay focused on outcomes—the *doing* of the day. Goals are important, but we must also develop collective social competence through learning and evolution. As we embark on the journey, we are always in relationship with others, especially in the work place. Business brings us together, yet we receive little or no training on how to relate and learn alongside others. Through life, we will encounter situations ranging from easy to very difficult, *whether we like it or not.* The choice we have is to embrace or reject any learning from our interactions. And it's time to choose evolution.

This is particularly true in intimate relationships and business relationships. With our business partners, as well as our intimate partners, we begin the process of awakening. Our relationships are the most powerful and accelerated paths of learning available. If we are closed to the wisdom that comes from being in relationship, our individual and collective evolution will suffer. These continuous interactions are the true feedback loop that keeps us engaged and offers growth.

This opportunity for evolution will be presented continually to us through the people that are a part of our lives. Everyone is a mirror for us. When you meet new people, as well as when you're working with new people, you are drawing into your life the very people who will provide you the opportunity to evolve. Rather than moving into survival mode and becoming defensive, ask yourself, "What is here for me to learn?" If in conflict, whether internal or external, will you wonder about what the other person is mirroring to you rather than grabbing onto the conflict? Will you see it as an opportunity to connect with the individual and discover something about yourself?

Every relationship interaction is an opportunity to learn. When learning is the priority of your journey, your experience will be much more fulfilling. This applies to your relationship with yourself, others, projects—even food and money. It applies to relationships with anything or anyone.

Even with the best of intentions, we fall into a trap believing, "I've finally arrived." After a certain amount of time, we get comfortable with our experience and knowledge. It's a powerful feeling to get over a steep learning curve and to feel as if, "I finally understand this," or "I know that already." The trap we fall into is, "I know the way," and then we shut down any learning. We hold a position that we already know the way to do things. We may know *a* way, but when we're open to growth and learning, the possibilities for connection and innovation are endless.

Willingness to replace old beliefs with new, higher resonating beliefs is at the core of breaking through limitations. Carol S. Dweck, in her book, *Mindset,* refers to growth versus fixed mindsets. "When you enter a mindset, you enter a new world. In one world—the world of fixed traits—success is about proving you are smart or talented, about validating yourself. In the other world—the world of changing qualities—it's about stretching yourself to learn something new. Developing yourself."[1]

It's easy to see how this applies today. Knowledge is the commodity now, as well as how we relate to each other. We can and will evolve past old patterns of behaviors that are no longer of service to us as individuals and as a species.

A senior executive, after twenty years, ended up being laid off because she didn't keep current with new trends; a team holding its position about the way the software should be coded, rather than collaborating with another team, caused major delays with the project; an executive kept switching companies every three years because he's never happy; a board of directors who couldn't reach decisions because each member wants it done their way; a young executive who is unhappy in spite of her promotions because she is unwilling to discover her commitment to blame. All of these experiences are missed opportunities to shatter old patterns which are no longer of service and can show us our potential blind spots.

Constant learning pays off. One company realized sales were dropping and discovered their business plan was outdated. Since then they have exceeded goals and keep growing. Another executive had difficulty retaining employees. After his review, he discovered he didn't provide clear roles and expectations. Now colleagues want to join his team. In fact, he is turning people away. A chief technical officer discovered he was affecting his ability to achieve results because he wanted everyone to like him. He has since established goals and is holding people accountable. Finally, companies are learning that hitting the numbers isn't enough. They are now investing in human capital and development.

Does it need to be argued that a culture of learning is important given that technology is impacting every aspect of our world? No one is shielded from this fact. Fundamental to technological advancements is the continued transition from manual labor to automation. Mankind will be confronted with more complex economic and moral questions as technology accelerates. It is necessary for our human evolution to keep up with technological evolution. This requires us to move past our caveman attitudes and be more evolved so our interactions can support these advances.

At ground level, we must be open to learning. This is a moment-to-moment choice. Many times, we shut down opportunities to grow, using phrases such as, "I've got that," or "Been there, done that." Another way we demonstrate this is through our body language—folded arms, crossed legs, looking down, and other closed postures. Becoming defensive when experiencing feedback from others or the environment is yet another way. No wonder we are closed. Most feedback isn't necessary.

Are you excited to learn from the situations you are presented with by consciously assessing your behavior in the moment? Are you open and curious versus being mildly interested or outwardly agreeing while inwardly disagreeing? These behaviors shut down the natural interactive loop between people. Ask powerful questions such as: *"What can I learn in this interaction?" "What can I learn from this person?" "We disagree right now, so what's here for me to learn?" "Is there an opportunity for me to drop some old belief and step into the truth?" "Where can I evolve here?"*

Evolution begins with a commitment to learning, a willingness in every moment as opposed to defending ourselves by stonewalling, explaining, justifying, withdrawing, blaming, etc. We put a lot of value on people with high IQs, but a high IQ does not mean someone has social competence and is open to evolving. Leaders and companies who can evolve have a great advantage over those who cannot.

You can think of learning in terms of a scale. High openness to learning looks like genuine curiosity, taking full responsibility for an issue, listening consciously, expressing appreciation for the messenger, and demonstrating an open posture. Low openness to learning looks like defending, showing polite interest outwardly while inwardly clinging to your point of view, explaining how the person has misperceived the situation, justifying why you are the way you are, why you acted the way you did, and even finding fault with the *way* the message is delivered. For example, an attitude of "I don't like the tone of voice you are using" closes off connection. A constant learner chooses to listen beyond the tone and focuses on what is being communicated—shifting her context to "what can I learn about my relationship to this particular tone of voice? Is there something in me that wants to be liberated or healed?" In the extreme, being closed to learning is blaming someone, attacking or threatening someone, projecting onto another, creating conflict, or making an abrupt departure.

Evolution will be sparked by opening to the fact that every moment is a chance to learn. Conscious human beings have access to new possibilities in their leadership, with their relationships and how they move through the world as they continue to grow.

The next time you talk about a culture of feedback, shift the discussion to a culture of evolution.

Applying the Practice and the Culture of Evolution

Step 1: Make the commitment to growth and learning as a way of life

Step 2: Ask "What is here for me to learn? Is there a chance for me to evolve?"

Step 3: Notice your posture; notice your thoughts. Are you open or closed?

Step 4: Get curious and stay curious—find the gem of wisdom

CREDIT —————————————————————

1 Dweck Ph.D., Carol. (2006). Mindset: The New Psychology of Success: How We Can Learn to Fulfill Our Potential. New York, NY. Ballantine. (p. 15)

CHAPTER 13

VALUES—THE CONGRUENT INDIVIDUAL

A conscious individual shows remarkable congruence between what he or she claims to stand for and how they live their life. So many of my clients are seeking fulfillment, and yet they don't know what it is they are seeking. They move from company to company, role to role, or project to project, only to find themselves back where they started, dissatisfied and longing for a more meaningful and impactful life and career.

The action step to fulfillment is to get into alignment with what is important to you—to get in alignment with your values. To show remarkable congruence with what you claim to stand for and how you are in the world is extremely nourishing. When not in alignment with our values, we're not showing up fully. We're saying one thing and doing another. We show up as someone we're not. We waste time and energy in unconscious action.

You must know what your own personal values are so can show up in alignment with what's important to you. I often get blank stares when asking clients, "What are your values?" Most people are uncertain what this question means. People have lost touch with what is important in their lives. You too may be asking, "What is a value?" It is a moral principle, action, activity, or belief that is important to you. A client of mine defined values as "concepts that represent how you want to live your life in a genuine way." In short, a value is what's important to you and what makes you happy. Ask yourself, what is it about you that if you took it away, you wouldn't know yourself or would feel extremely dissatisfied?

Committing time to your values increases your daily fulfillment. Integrating your values into your executive presence has a phenomenal impact on your work life and makes you a more effective and inspirational leader. When you're clear about your values, it gives easy prioritization to your daily tasks. I highly value being in nature, so I chose to live in the Bay Area where I have easy access to hiking trails, and beaches; I also value transparency, which makes me an open book for people.

Be clear about your values; then you can manage the tension that arises when are asked to step out of them. For example, I have a value for open communication and transparency. As I communicate, I make sure I am open and transparent. However, as leaders, we can't always disclose all the information we have, such as cases concerning insider information. In my leadership roles in financial services, I keep my value for transparency in alignment by saying, "I am not able to disclose that information now, and as soon as I can, I will communicate it." By not trying to make something up about the situation (which would have been out of alignment), I was able to be congruent with who I am. Similarly, although I am transparent, I respect my clients' confidentiality when reviewing a coaching project with their manager. The aim is not to keep secrets but to protect privacy and confidentiality of the individual client. I inform the manager that while I believe in open communication, the individual session content is confidential.

Many people don't even know what their values are, and in the absence of consciously aligning with what's important to them, they tend to absorb their values from others. They take on their parents' values, a set of cultural or religious values, a company's values, all while not being mindful if the value is even important to *them*. Consequently, they end up being out of alignment and feel like an imposter. Their self-esteem is diminished. Being congruent is crucial to being a successful leader, and it is obvious when a leader doesn't act for what they stand for.

As I said previously, once you make conscious decisions about that which is important, you can navigate the tension that is created with others when values don't match. For instance, you'll have a set of values, and your company will have a set of values. It's very rare that 100 percent of your values match your company's values. Usually, there are one or two key values that don't match up, and this creates tension. That's okay and is normal, but it's important to be conscious of this so that your effectiveness as an individual or leader isn't diminished. You can acknowledge, "I create tension in myself because I'm out of alignment with one of my company's values." It's important to know how to navigate through the tension and emotions that arise. Trying to be someone you're not is an immense energy drain. When you can navigate the tension and emotions, you can respond appropriately and be true to who you are.

I have numerous clients who want to change jobs or leave their companies because they're not happy. I call this the "grass is greener" effect, jumping to another role or company to try to be more fulfilled. If you aren't clear about what's important, you will never be satisfied. For instance, I have a client, a senior executive, who wanted to quit his job and go to another company. This was the third time in six years he wanted to do this. Here is our conversation.

Abby: "Well, do you know what your values are?"

Client: "Well, what do you mean?"

Abby: "What's important to you about the type of company you work for or the day-to-day of the role you are in or are considering? How much time do you spend in the activities that are important to you?"

Client: "You know, I don't know."

If he were to switch jobs again, he would just recreate the same misery and unsatisfying life. Immediately we determined his values so that he was clearer about what kind of role he wanted. His current role was providing everything he wanted, except for a couple of minor things, and he could add these experiences in his role at his current company, into his day-to-day workflow. He had a role that was fit him well, and it was just a matter of realizing this.

Another client was running on autopilot. He had unconsciously absorbed the values of others. Once we established his values, we learned that work/life flexibility is essential to him. He wanted to work from home one day a week, to leave by 5 p.m. another day of the week, and turn off technology one day on the weekend. Once he was clear about what was important to him, he could maneuver his workflow to make sure he got out the door in time to go home and spend time with his baby, etc. Before he implemented this practice, he was miserable.

Not aligning with values was one of my client's issues. This a senior executive who loves to travel because he enjoyed new experiences in new locations. This was very important to him and his fulfillment. But he was not conscious of this value, and his effectiveness at work was declining. He asked for coaching regarding his executive effectiveness.

After a few sessions, I said to him, "That is about the sixth time I've heard about travel. It's clear that it is very important to you. When was the last time you took a trip?" He replied, "It's been a year." We identified that travel is a value he wasn't incorporating into his life—professional or personal—we immediately planned for him to take day trips with his wife on the weekends at least once a month. He now takes all his vacation time and, when possible, his wife goes along on business trips, even staying an extra day in the location just for fun. As soon as he began bringing his love of travel back into his life, his effectiveness at work returned to its normal level, and he received feedback that he was even more energetic and enthusiastic.

Live Consciously and Make a List of Values

You may be asking, *"How do I determine what my values are?"* This is a simple process and doesn't require you to go on some intense retreat or sabbatical to find yourself. Take out a sheet of paper and start brainstorming what's important to you. You can ask things like *"What's important to me?" "What are the things that I enjoy doing?"* For instance, what is something that you enjoy so much that if you didn't do it, you wouldn't recognize yourself? What were you doing during the times you were most happy, most proud, most fulfilled and satisfied? What were you doing and what factors contributed to your state? What parts of your life do you value? Make it easy on yourself and write everything down that comes to you. It's that simple. Begin to map out what is important to you in your day-to-day life and how you can implement them.

I value organization, so my home is neat and orderly. I also value open-mindedness, so I surround myself with open-minded people. Because I value sustainability, I've eliminated as much plastic in my life as I can and switched from paper towels to cloth napkins, slowly eradicating harmful chemical cleansers and converting to ones that don't harm the environment. My car is a hybrid. I am getting in alignment with my value of caring for the planet and being a producer versus a consumer. Becoming more congruent, I feel complete, more satisfied, more fulfilled.

Act to Align with Your Values

Once you've established your list, here is the big question: how many minutes per day do you actively participate in these things that are important to you? Regarding fulfillment, this is where the rubber meets the road. Once you know your values, you may rearrange your activities around what's important to you. Getting off autopilot can be an experience, so go easy. In other words, you may begin to realize you've been organizing your life around what's *not* important to you. This can be a shock. Be compassionate with yourself.

In the Workplace

How does this affect teams and organizations? Everyone has his or her own set of values. One might have a value for autonomy when working on a project while another may value collaboration. This can cause tension and must be recognized consciously. It's okay to say, "You have your values, I have mine." You can consciously navigate through the emotions that arise. You may notice it and say, "I don't have a value for working autonomously on this project," "I'd rather work together." Then you have a conversation about emotions and decide what to do collaboratively, rather than just realizing there is tension and not knowing what to do with it. You consciously create your process together, rather than ignore the tension.

For people with whom you work, you'll begin to learn their values. It's helpful to know your own *and* others' so you can co-create an experience which serves everyone, especially with your spouse, close intimate relationships, and those with whom you work. Knowing what your partner's values are versus your own is critical since there's always a gap. That's when tension is created. It's similar with your close colleagues. (Sometimes we spend more time with our colleagues than our partners at times.) Similar circumstances exist with your company's values. There is always a gap, and the skills is to learn how to navigate the gap by bringing it forward consciously. Then we realize it's not because we're disagreeable, it's because we don't have a similar value around a topic, and there's always a collective solution.

The innovative and creative organizations of the world want you to be in alignment with your values. They recognize that fulfilled employees increase productivity and profitability. When you are fulfilled, profits go up, so they will let you create a role at their organization if it's in alignment with the vision of the company.

How can you create more satisfaction in your roles in your day-to-day life at work and home?

Applying the Practice: Be a Congruent Human—Identify Your Values

Step 1: Grab pen and paper and brainstorm what's important to you.

Step 2: Write down ways to implement these activities in your life.

Step 3: Navigate any emotions and tension that arise from value misalignments.

CHAPTER 14

LEADERSHIP QUALITY— THE CONGRUENT LEADER

What is your leadership style? What are the characteristics and values that make up your leadership style, your brand? No matter what, if you're walking to the restroom, to the micro kitchen, presenting in front of your board of directors, talking to a front-line person, are you showing up in your own leadership style, congruently, all the time, in every moment? Are you moving with a purpose?

As a leader, you develop character, a brand. Companies have brands, and you have your own. Steve Jobs had a brand. Mark Zuckerberg has a brand. You have a brand. What is yours? Just like values, in the absence of consciously developing your brand around the truth of who you are, you will take on others' characteristics. And again, *trying to be someone you are not is an immense energy drain.*

There are likely some positive and negative aspects of your brand. Steve Jobs had a very creative, innovative, visionary brand. He also had the brand of not being so good with his employees. Barack Obama has a brand. He's clear, articulate, intelligent, a Nobel Prize winner—aspects that are all part of his brand. It's important always to be consciously true to your brand; a conscious leader is a congruent leader *and* a human being.

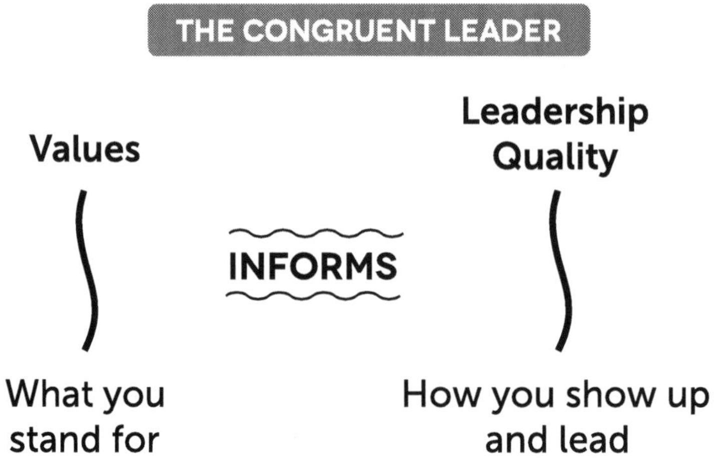

THE CONGRUENT LEADER

Values

Leadership
Quality

〉

∼∼∼∼
INFORMS
∼∼∼∼

〉

What you
stand for

How you show up
and lead

Figure 8

How Do I Determine My Own Leadership Quality?

There are a few ways to determine your leadership brand. One is getting in alignment with your values. Another is the constant feedback you hear back from people. In the absence of anything at all, consciously develop your brand.

Ask Yourself These Questions When Consciously Creating Your Quality

- What resonates with you?
- What's the type of leadership you want to provide?
- What do you want to stand for as a leader?
- What do you repeatedly hear from people throughout the years?
- What are those qualities you aspire to?
- What is your point of view that is a hallmark of who you are?

It's important to capture this on paper. Make a list to refer to because you *will* drift out of your brand when you drift from presence. We all do. It's a part of the human condition. Your brand will develop over time as you grow and develop as a human being and leader, as will your ability to be true to it.

Be conscious about the brand you want to create. Some of it will come out naturally through introspective discovery. Some aspects may come through experiences. If you keep hearing from people that they trust you, it's very likely that trust, or some aspect of it, is part of your brand, and it's time to own it.

The Space Between—Be Congruent with the Truth

When you are interacting with others, what you are putting in the space between you and others, verbally and nonverbally, must be congruent with your values and your brand—in alignment with the truth of who you are. If you are not in alignment with who you are, the real you, immediately you lose presence and connection with yourself and others. This is relevant for you in one-on-one conversations, when you are interacting with a group, and when you are presenting to thousands.

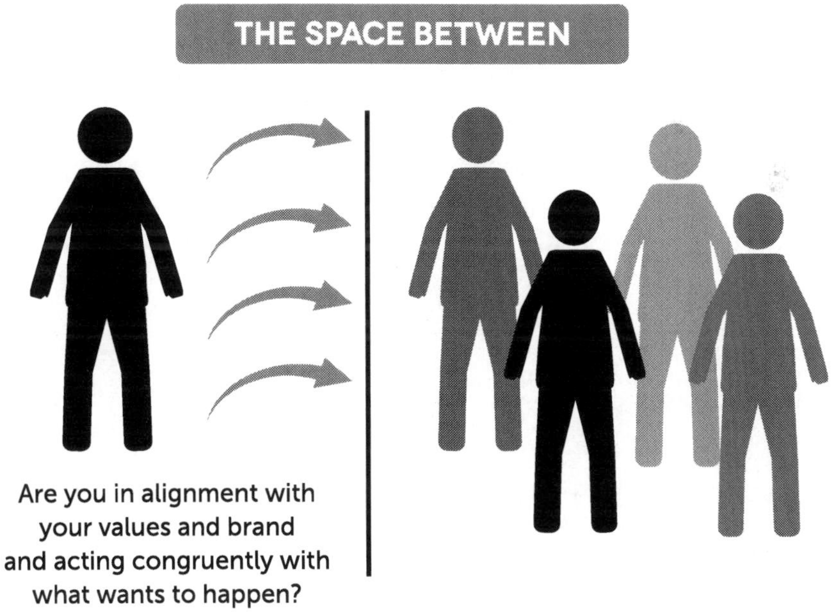

THE SPACE BETWEEN

Are you in alignment with
your values and brand
and acting congruently with
what wants to happen?

Figure 9

When you are out of alignment with the truth of who you are, your consciousness knows it, and everyone else can feel it as well. Immediately tension fills the air. You've likely experienced this. Think of the person who walks into the room and the whole room shifts. The room can lift or fall depending on the congruence of the leader. Here is the simple reason why: we are all connected.

How We Act Affects Others

Mirror neurons are always communicating and sending out frequencies. Our mirror neurons are always firing. The University of Parma, Italy studied this concept with monkeys.1 When electrodes were placed in a monkey's brain, researchers found that the monkey's neurons fired when performing the activity as well as when *watching* another monkey perform the activity. It is suggested that these mirror neurons exist in humans too. Each of us will grab onto another's neurons unless we are mindful about our own. In short, whatever type of energy, emotion, or state we are projecting, there's a chance that another will mirror it back and you may be absorbing someone else's brand. This is how a person can walk into a room and shift the energy.

It's important to bring conscious awareness to what are you putting into the space between you and the other person. That is, what is coming out of your mouth? How are you acting?

What's your non-verbal communication? Are you speaking and moving about the world with a purpose? Are you acting in accordance with your values and that for which you claim to stand? If you're with someone else, and especially if you're with numerous people and none of them are present, your neurons are going to want to grab onto that drama or state. If they're gossiping, your neurons are going to want to grab onto that. If someone is acting out of fear, you may quickly jump to fear. You have a choice. You don't have to mirror that. When you're mindful about it, you can consciously choose.

Choose Consciously

To live into your full potential, it's important that you're clear about what you want to throw in the space between you and others. Be conscious about how you want to infuse your neurons to help other people or situations to shift. What does this look like? We've all experienced being in a room when someone walks in and the whole room shifts. That person can be you. We can shift the energy of an encounter, a group, or an entire room by being aware of and *intentional* with the energy we're bringing in.

What's your intention when you walk into a room? Do you want to walk into a meeting showing up in your full power? Do you want to bring love into the space when in a conflict with a spouse or colleague? Do you want to bring connection, collaboration, and creativity into your interactions with your team on a project? Do you want to bring curiosity into a project meeting in conflict? This simple concept may not always seem easy. It is a practice, and you can increase your skill over time.

In every interaction, in every moment, how are you showing up? What you transmit into the space between you and others can be especially valuable with difficult conversations and conflict resolution. If you interact with the (many times unconscious) intention of grabbing onto someone else's point of view, you will. If you interact with the intention that you want to create collaboration, curiosity, and to be real and authentic, you will. You increase your skillfulness as you practice and increase your awareness.

For example, if someone approaches you, angry, fearful, or antagonistic, you can ask yourself, "How am I going to choose to respond in this moment, no matter what the other person is doing or saying?" This applies to all relationships. Do not separate work and personal. This is how you can create brilliant and intimate interactions. Step up fully and make the conscious choice to move with a purpose and act in alignment with your brand and values always. Be the congruent human being and leader at work and home.

Get Your Neurons Firing and Establish Your Container

A container is what any interaction is infused with. Imagine someone in a jar with you. A jar is a physical container. Your interactions are contained within that jar. The container might be a board meeting, a team meeting, a project, a one-on-one meeting, a company culture, or a relationship. What do you want your company culture infused with? What's the baseline that you can always reference? Be mindful so that you're moving through the world, as an individual and an organization, in a container that you know you want. My container is full of love, appreciation, celebration and gratitude, connection, innovation, and productivity. I don't want my container to be drama, holding a position, shutting down innovation, unproductive workload, or drama. When you notice that you don't want it to be something, that's a great pivot point; then look at what you *do* want, and be very intentional about with what you infuse your interactions.

No matter what's happening for the people on the other side of you, in any encounter (whether it is with one person, five, or ten), you can be intentional with your response and choose from your container. If people on your team are all in drama about a project, you can consciously decide how you want to respond, both verbally and non-verbally. Get your neurons firing with your brand. When this is your norm, it doesn't matter if you are in a meeting, presenting to hundreds of people, or in the check-out line at the grocery store. With practice, you can move with a purpose always. Lead yourself, and you can lead others.

The Leader Sets the Tone

Another way to say this myself is "What is my tone of behavior as I go about the world?" My baseline is love, compassion, learning, understanding, and gratitude. I walk into every meeting with that intention. I ask myself, how can I exude gratitude, so that's what my neurons are firing? Before I walk into a meeting, I ask, "What can I celebrate right now? How I show gratitude right now? What can I learn?" As I think about the answers to these questions, I'm preparing my neurons. Then, when I walk in, people go, "Wow!" It's because they can feel my brand. Imagine the tone of a tension-filled meeting if you come with a baseline of compassion; think about the increased productivity and collaboration. Right away, people shift out of drama by being intentional with the energy of how *you* walk in. This happens very naturally right before any interaction when you breathe and step into your preferred state.

Determine what type of energy you want to transmit? Make a conscious decision. I suggest love, appreciation, gratitude, and wisdom. And from a business standpoint, I add curiosity, presence, learning, and productivity. The more you are in alignment, in both your personal and business life, the more effective and integrated it will be; *and this can produce amazing results.*

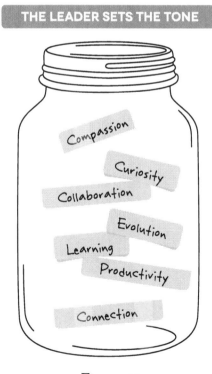

Figure 10

Applying the Practice: Be a Congruent Leader—Your Leadership Quality

Step 1: Identify if your brand is in alignment with your values.

Step 2: Make a list of what you stand for as a leader; write it down and reference it.

Step 3: Fill your container with your preferred transmissions.

Step 4: Establish your baseline for interactions.

Step 5: Breathe and create the state within you before all interactions.

CREDIT ———————————————————

1 Tan, Chade-Meng. (2012). Search Inside Yourself: The Unexpected path to Achieving Success, Happiness (and World Peace). New York, NY. Harper Collins

CHAPTER 15

STYLE DIFFERENCES

One of the ways we create conflict with each other is we don't try to understand how their style preferences differ from ours. Instead of understanding and appreciating them, we complain because people aren't "doing it the way that I want." I am continually amazed at how much the misunderstanding of style differences derails projects, relationships, teams, and communication between people. It's as if this list is endless. While this seems elementary, we are not taught what our preferences are. I go out of my way to explain this to young people to empower them with advantage as they enter the workforce.

I am not going to spend a lot of time here. We need to be conscious of our style preferences and the way they impact how we relate and collaborate. Style differences come into play regarding *how* we get things done, *how* we relate from a very tactical level. If we find that we are not working well with someone at a tactical level, chances are our styles are clashing, especially if we find we are struggling in conversations with a colleague.

The framework that helps determine your style is very helpful, including diagnostic tools. With some basic conscious awareness, we can optimize for style differences rather than create drama. Here are some basic style preferences:

Problem-Solving Aptitude—Solving for X

Diagnostic Reasoning. Quickly seeing the relationship between apparently unrelated facts and forming an accurate conclusion from a few scattered bits of evidence

Analytical Reasoning. Quickly organizing concepts, information, or things in a logical sequence

Our Natural Way of Understanding the World Around Us Can Differ

Spatial: Inborn talent for understanding, working easily with three-dimensional reality, concerned with thinking about or working directly with "things"

Tangibles: Concern with tangibles, three-dimensional not required, physical evidence, and change of tangible events play important roles, hands-on, day-to-day management

Non-spatial: Gifted in understanding nonphysical, conceptual reality

Abstract: Theoretical or concept-oriented, tangible results in the world of physical reality is not required

Concrete: Driven to seek concrete results

Learn to Be Different

Visual: Use photos, pictures, images, and visual aids, including charts, graphs, and instructions

Auditory: Use sound via words, speaking, and listening

Kinesthetic: Learn through experience; dive right in, using the body, hands, and sense of touch, learn through action; this may seem unorganized when it's trial-by-error type learning

Know Your Orientation—Energy is Crucial to Collaboration

Extraversion: "In the extraverted attitude, energy and attention flow out, or are drawn out, to the objects and people in the environment. The individual experiences a desire to act on the environment, to affirm its importance, to increase its effect. Persons habitually taking the Extraverted attitude may develop some or all the characteristics associated with Extraversion: awareness of and reliance on the environment for stimulation and guidance; an eagerness to interact with the outer world; an action-oriented, sometimes impulsive way of meeting life; openness to new experiences; ease of communication and sociability; and a desire to 'talk things out.'"[1]

Introversion: "In the Introverted attitude, energy is drawn from the environment toward inner experience and reflection. One desires to stay focused on the internal, subjective state, to affirm its value, and to maintain this focus if possible. The main interests of the Introverted type are in the world of concepts, ideas, and inner experiences. Persons habitually taking the Introverted attitude may develop some or all the characteristics associated with Introversion: interest in the clarity of concepts, ideas, and recollected experience; reliance on enduring concepts and experiences more than on transitory external events or fleeting ideas; a thoughtful, contemplative detachment; an enjoyment of solitude and privacy; and a desire to "think things out" before talking about them."[2]

General Lifestyles Differ

Values + Strengths	=	*What* we prefer to do
Style Preferences	=	*How* we prefer to do it
What + How	=	Impact, contribution, and fulfillment

Figure 11

Closed-ended: Decisive, planned and orderly, preferring structure and control, closure

Open-ended: Flexible, adaptable, spontaneous, preferring keeping options open

Preferred Work Styles Differ

Tribal: Feels at home as part of a group either out in front or behind the scenes

Maestro: Independent-minded mavericks who walk to the beat of a different drummer, feeling like an outsider, rarely joining groups, and would rather not collaborate to get the job done

Competitive Equilibrium Continuum

Create: To cause to come into being, as something unique that would not naturally evolve or that is not made by ordinary processes. To evolve from one's own thought or imagination. The ability to invent, to create that which did not exist before. True creativity involves a paradigm change, a transformation and a new way of perceiving or understanding.

Sustain: To keep up, to keep going, as an action or process

Destroy: To put an end to, or complete

This is not an exhaustive list of style preferences. Furthermore, none of these are better than the other. We each have our preferences, our preferred way of how we like to get things done. We default to our preferences.

You have probably heard about the importance of being in your strengths. Playing to your strengths *is* essential. Similarly, as I mentioned, aligning with your values is equally important. I think about it this way:

Apply Conscious Knowledge

My preferences are as follows: diagnostic reasoning, non-spatial, abstract, kinesthetic and visual, introversion, open-ended, maestro, create and destroy. Now with these preferences, you'd hardly think I belong in sales leadership, where I spend the bulk of my career. I am more the profile of serial entrepreneur or a software engineer. Previously I stated that presence is the foundation for everything. Because I know my style preferences, I can be present with myself, notice what is required of me in the moment and exercise different muscles. It's *never always* the time to be any one of any of the above preferences.

Comments from others early on in life: "I want to hear more from you. You don't share what's going on for you." Because I am aware of my powerful preference for introversion, in this recognition, I brought conscious attention to my leadership and learned how to exercise my extravert muscles. I learned to speak up more and to find satisfaction in being around others. Other comments from others early on in life: "Why can't you plan anything? Can't we just decide what we are doing?" Because of my preference for being open-ended, I learned early on in life that this is not helpful for achieving goals. Furthermore, friends were frustrated with my because I never enjoyed planning anything—wanting instead to "go with the flow." I learned that bringing things to closure creates more freedom for new ideas and spontaneous action.

Because I know my preference for kinesthetic and visual learning, I watch out for clients who are auditory learners. I make sure to speak more and explain things clearly so they can more easily understand what I am teaching. I struggled in school when any teacher lectured. It's now how I prefer to learn, and I easily became bored. To this day, I prefer holding a book and seeing it versus audio books that I must listen to. Our educational system is set up for mediocrity. We could benefit from entertaining the idea that we should be teaching children how to learn. This skill will benefit them throughout their lifetime.

Why They Do That

Recognition of style differences directly invites compassion, understanding, and the agility to respond in the moment to what is being asked of you. You are invited into constant learning by learning from others that which you are not able to see because of your own preferences. You will expose others to different ways of being which invites them to evolve new and different muscles. We all benefit. Furthermore, on a fundamental level, we all have different styles, therefore it's crucial to realize this, and meet your audience in any given situation.

Misunderstanding style differences derails projects, relationships, teams, and communication between people. A comment such as, "So that's why they always do that!" is always welcome. Instead of drama, let the learning begin.

CREDIT ─────────────────────────

1,2 Myers, Isabel Briggs. McCaulley, Mary H. Quenk, Naomi L. Hammer, Allen L. (2003) MBTI Manual: A Guide to the Development and Use of The Myers-Briggs Type Indicator. Third Edition. Mountain View, CA. CPP, Inc. (p. 26)

CHAPTER 16

THE POWER OF BREATH AND MOVEMENT

Two very important activities in support of your nervous system are breath and movement. When we are not breathing deeply to get enough oxygen, and when we are not moving, our physiology is fighting us, and our vitality suffers. Crucial to letting your emotional energy flow is your ability to be aware of your nervous system and how much breath and movement it needs to support your activities.

Breathing is Important

The benefits to increasing your body's oxygen flow are nothing short of amazing. Mark Matousek talks about the effects of breathing on our health in his article, 'Is the Way You Breathe Bad for Your Health?" He states, "Chinese and yogis have long stated the importance of breathing, and science is finally catching up. Newborns come into the world breathing deeply, and as we age stress takes over, and we start breathing shallowly. By adulthood, we are taking 15 to 20 breaths per minute—three to four times faster than is optimal. That's where the trouble can start."

In the same article, "Rapid, shallow breathing sends a message to our adrenal glands that we're in fight-or-flight mode, and they begin pumping out stress hormones like Cortisol," explains Brenda Stockdale, director of mind-body medicine at the RC Cancer Centers in Atlanta. "And when the body is stressed, it's weakened. Our immune cells normally function like 'little Pac-Men,'" Stockdale explains, "patrolling for and destroying bacteria and diseased cells before they can multiply. But when cortisol levels are elevated, those immune cells slow down drastically, allowing pathogens and diseased cells to slip by."[1] If you slow your breath down, and exhale, you engage your parasympathetic nervous system, and you can't get anxious.

We release 70 percent of the toxins in our bodies through our breath. The less you're breathing, the fewer toxins you're releasing and the more toxins you're keeping in your body that lead to illnesses.

Your cognition needs oxygen to develop. Your brain uses twenty percent of the oxygen in your body, three times more than your muscles. As you breathe more consciously and bring more oxygen into your brain, your cognition will be optimized. There is an infinite amount of science and research that I am not going to review here. If you'd like to know more, there are volumes of scientific information you can find easily on the web.

Throughout your day, breathing deeply into your belly is highly important. This is a paradigm shift; we're taught to wear tight clothing and suck our stomachs in. This is detrimental to our well-being. It's important to relax your belly so that your diaphragm can do its job. You want all the oxygen you can get into your body and brain to fuel yourself into your highest level of activity. When you slow your breathing, you are breathing *consciously* and allowing your nervous system to sustain your activities.

Breathing increases your awareness and assists you in allowing waves of emotion to move through you rapidly. When you hold your breath, or if your breath is shallow, you immediately lose presence and head straight into drama. Fear and anger will likely arise as your body fills with stale air and CO^2. At any time, you're only one or two exhales and a body posture shift away from a state of flow.

When facilitating workshops, to prove this point, I will instruct everyone hold their breath for a minute or breathe shallowly and repeat their name. At sixty seconds, everyone is furious or feeling contracted. Then I instruct them to exhale fully, then inhale deeply—three sets. Then I instruct them to notice how they feel. The difference is remarkable.

Another example drives home the importance of breathing in supporting your nervous system and brain power. In workshops, I have the group solve for Problem X, a real problem they are dealing with. While clients are sitting still and in their "normal" states of breathing, I facilitate a brainstorming session for solving "X." I record their responses on a flip chart or whiteboard. Then I instruct them to get up and consciously breathe while moving about the room. To emphasize the point, I instruct them to move in ways that are unfamiliar to them. While they are breathing and moving, I instruct them to solve for "X" again, the same exact problem. Again, I capture their ideas on a second flip chart or whiteboard. I have them stop to look at the two flip charts. The difference between them is remarkable. The first flip chart is littered with negativity, constriction, and how "we can't do it." The second flip chart is loaded with innovative solutions and possibilities. Everyone in the room is astounded—even me. It never ceases to surprise me at the difference in idea flow.

Move Around

Move your body as much as possible, in as many ways as possible. Our psychological patterns get locked in our muscular tensions. The less we move, the more our thoughts take over, and the more likely we will create conflict. If we frequently move throughout our day, we'll be more relaxed and present. Harvard Business Review printed an article called *Sitting Is the Smoking of Our Generation* by Nilofer Merchant which iterated that long periods of sitting are more detrimental to health than smoking. More people die of obesity from sitting, which slows metabolism, than from the effects of smoking.[2]

There is a reason that many organizations are adopting new and innovative workspace. There are workplaces where people can move while they're working on projects. Companies now have ping pong tables available or walking paths on the premises. Many companies now offer standing desks, a sign of a laid-back culture; but it's more than that. Movement supports a healthy nervous system. Even while writing this book, I alternate between sitting down and writing at a standing desk. At the 60-minute mark, I make sure to stop and move around. The entire time, I am focused on deep breathing.

It is important to pay attention to *how* we're moving. When we are born, we have thousands of potential joint movements our bodies can make. As we grow older, we lose flexibility because we've stopped using the range of movement in our joints. Drastically constricting ourselves in our movement, we become stiff like boards. Adults carry more muscle mass, adding to the stiffness, but that muscle mass can be lost through inactivity. All of this contributes to poor posture and back issues. If we make a practice of moving our bodies in new and different ways, we can access creativity, intellect, and increase our energy and vitality.

Applying the Practice: Supporting the Nervous System with Breathing

Step 1: Check your breathing—is your breathing shallow or into your belly?

Step 2: If breathing into your belly, keep it up.

Step 3: If it's shallow, empty your lungs with a big exhale, then breathe.

Step 4: Proactively breathe into your belly.

By focusing on the exhale, we empty our lungs of CO_2, and then the inhale is easier. By exhaling, we engage our parasympathetic nervous system.

Applying the Practice: Supporting the Nervous System with Moving

Step 1: Check your posture.

Step 2: Move in ways that are uncommon to you to open your joints.

Stand up and sit down.

Shake limbs a bit.

Twiddle fingers.

Rotate wrists and ankles.

Go for a quick walk down the hall and back.

Move facial muscles in a way to loosen the jaw.

Step 3: Proactively move throughout the day.

CREDIT ————————————————

1 Matousek, M. From the November 2011 issue of O, The Oprah Magazine, Is the Way You Breathe Bad for Your Health? Retrieved from www.oprah.com/spirit/Deep-Breathing-Methods- How-Breathing-Reduces-Stress

2 Merchant, Nilofer. (2013, January 14). Sitting Is the Smoking of Our Generation.

CHAPTER 17

CONSCIOUS AGREEMENTS

In our personal and professional lives, we navigate our daily activities through a series of agreements. Holding ourselves accountable to the agreements we make builds trust, enhances our self-efficacy, and keeps us very productive.

Whereas a commitment is a pact with the universe, an agreement is a contract between two or more people where they do what they say they will do. Agreements include what time to start a meeting, choosing who will pick up the kids, negotiating deadlines on projects, and of course, formal written contracts. We experience an easy feeling when an agreement is kept. Think about how refreshing it is when people show up to meetings on time or do what they say they will do.

On the other hand, think about your experience when people are late to meetings or don't follow through with something they said they would do. The results are devastating. Meetings start late, and the people who are on time usually feel angry. This creates a group of disconnected individuals. Part of a project is not completed as promised, and it slows the entire process. Productivity lags and trust erodes.

This phenomenon doesn't just happen with others. We must hold ourselves accountable for our actions and goals. Self-efficacy is a necessary agent for high self-esteem—having a strong self-concept affords us richer relationships. We learn to trust our own actions with clear agreements. By setting clear agreements with ourselves, we can measure our progress against our goals and adjust accordingly when necessary. Agreements are simple, but not always easy. The overriding context of conscious agreements is to *act in good faith*. In business and personal relationships to act in good faith is a genuine intention to be fair, open and honest with others regardless of any outcome. To act in good faith and fair dealing requires a level of maturity and emotional intelligence because asking for a clear agreement doesn't always mean you will get what you want. It's about having the maturity to agree to disagree, then to agree on action steps after. It also means taking responsibility for your part even when things don't go your way.

Even when you make an agreement that is not necessarily important to you—but is important to others—the agreement needs to be kept, avoiding tension and conflict. People can tell if you are engaged or not and if you want to participate. When you are not engaged, you lose presence and are not fully collaborating—therefore slowing progress.

Furthermore, just because you have an agreement in place, doesn't mean the other party will necessarily follow-through on it. Conscious leaders follow through on their part and act in good faith—*regardless* of others' actions. This is a choice point of who you want to be in the world and staying in alignment with your brand.

Years ago, I formed a Limited Liability Company (LLC) with another individual. We had a formal written document created—a very clear set of agreements—an actual contract. As part of the contract, we agreed to make an initial equal capital contribution so that our ownership was 50/50.

The other person never made the capital contribution. Immediately the agreement was unconsciously broken and against good faith. I did not blame or shame the other person. However, I initiated the discussion and requested that she keep her part of the agreement. This was a red flag of course and a series of other broken agreements eroded the relationship and we closed the LLC. At the end of the experience I felt satisfied because I kept the agreements and acted in good faith for my part.

Another example is when we are deciding on a course of action with regard to a project. We may not agree to disagree on a course, but we must agree on the action steps and follow-through. We can't always do things the way we want, however, it's important for the relationship and the culture of the organization to be united in those action steps. Being conscious that everyone gets a chance to have their idea implemented creates a culture of learning.

Why Don't We Make Clear Agreements?

It is not a standard conscious practice to create clear agreements. There are numerous reasons why.

Lazy or sloppy interactions. The way we work now is very different. Everything is moving at a very rapid pace, and it's easy to end a meeting or conversation without clear deliverables.

Agreements are scary. When you make an agreement, you are saying that you will do it and hold yourself accountable to that action. Clear agreements invite responsibility. This level of interaction *does* require maturity and follow-through.

We choose to be reactive rather than proactive. When we make clear agreements, we are proactively navigating our time. By not establishing clarity, we wait for people to show up or for the next event to happen. We are *reacting* to life rather than directly *interacting* with life. In the workforce, this is highly counterproductive. I hear frequently from clients that they have too many meetings.

Style differences. Open-ended individuals tend to avoid bringing things to closure. They like to go with the flow. For them, clear agreements feel stressful. Closed-ended individuals typically love deadlines which are very important for moving an objective forward. If you find yourself struggling to create a clear agreement with someone, it could be a style difference. Bring out your compassion and discuss the importance of deadlines. No matter what your personality style may be, not making clear agreements is an absolute energy drain on everyone.

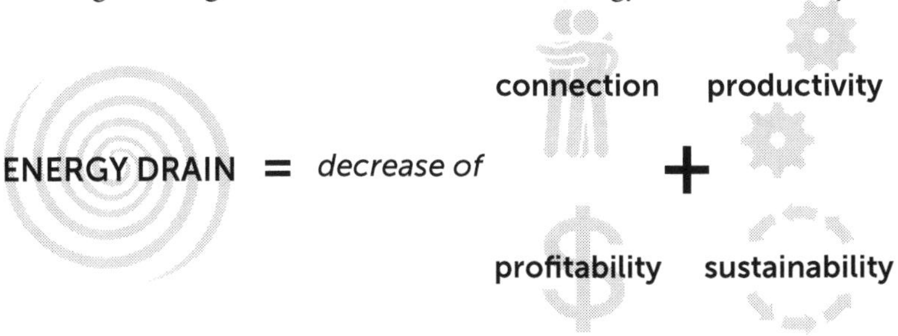

ENERGY DRAIN = *decrease of* connection + productivity + profitability + sustainability

Figure 12

The myth that agreements take away freedom. Most people believe agreements are binding instead of being an initial contract. They feel confined and imprisoned by their agreements, rather than seeing the benefit of agreements and the freedom they offer. There is some truth to this. By holding ourselves accountable, we might feel a wave of fear, and many people avoid fear when they can. Entering into an agreement brings self-accountability to the forefront and may put us on edge. For example, agreeing to have the final draft of a presentation to your CEO by an exact date can bring up a lot of fear. The agreement is like putting a stake in the ground and saying that you will have it done by a certain time. Internally you might feel scared because it's your first interaction or presentation with the CEO.

The trap of saying yes to everything. Saying yes to everything is just as ineffective as not creating an agreement. It is easier to not to agree than it is to get out of an agreement you don't want to keep. Ideally, make only agreements that you *want* to make. Consider the example of the individual who says yes to everything—the consummate Hero. Another example is the individual who sets up the networking luncheon and really doesn't want to network with the other individual. Rather than consciously saying no, they agree to go, then they're late or they cancel at the last, minute wreaking havoc on their brand and inviting self-deprecation.

Not knowing how to make, keep, and change agreements. Most people have never been taught how to create clear agreements. In some places, accountability is punished. Some leaders do not harness the power of clear deadlines, using the excuse, "I like to go with the flow." Furthermore, these leaders aren't open to learning; they're not seeing the benefit of clear agreements and how they dramatically increase productivity. Navigating gracefully and effectively through agreements saves time and energy. Keep track through a system. Write them down, or use a task list or a calendar. "I forgot" isn't a valid excuse—be exceptional.

Realize the power of *no*. *No* is the new yes. It is imperative that we realize the power of *no*. With immediate access to information readily at our fingertips, discerning your true *yes* and *no* will keep you from becoming distracted. We all have an overflowing plate of situations, and even if we worked twenty-four hours a day, seven days a week, the plate would still be overloaded. Fear of missing out rears its ugly head, and we feel overwhelmed. We want to do everything.

You will experience more vitality when you start to honor what's important to you, and start to say *no*. As we are clearer in our *no*, we create more power in our *yes*. Dr. Travis Bradberry stated that successful people ". . . won't say yes unless they really want to. Research conducted at the University of California in San Francisco shows that the more difficulty that you have saying *no*, the more likely you are to experience stress, burnout, and even depression. Saying *no* is indeed a major challenge for most people. *No* is a powerful word that you should not be afraid to wield. When it's time to say it, emotionally intelligent people avoid phrases like, "I don't think I can," or "I'm not certain." Saying *no* to a new agreement honors your existing agreements and gives you the opportunity to successfully fulfill them."

How to Navigate Clear Agreements

Ask for a clear agreement—consciously. Use these simple questions: *How much? Of what? By when? By whom?* We rarely ask for these specifics and usually end a meeting without deliverables or clear next steps. This is especially true when ending tough conversations. We are so pleased that we made it through a hard conversation, we forget to create accountability. Make this a habit.

Follow through. Do what you say you will do by the agreed upon deadline.

Change agreements consciously. In a fast-moving world and innovative environment, situations change. Life happens, and when it does, it's okay to change an agreement, but do so *consciously*. Tell the truth about your experience and provide some facts as to why you are requesting the change. Listen to the other person's experience and communications, and then negotiate another agreement. Learn from your experience by identifying the source of the broken agreement so that you hone your skills.

Break agreements consciously. Acknowledge to the concerned people as soon as possible that you cannot fulfill your part of the agreement. Take responsibility for breaking the agreement by letting go of accusations, justifications, and defenses. Listen to responses from others about how it affects their situation. Let everyone involved have their experience. Ask what you can do to address any consequences of breaking the agreement. Remember that fear will arise when changing or breaking an agreement—therefore breathe.

Return to constant learning. Again, learn from your experience. Do you recognize any pattern? Do you regularly change agreements? Allow time and space to hear and feel any feelings with regard to broken and changed agreements. If you find yourself continually changing or breaking agreements, chances are you aren't *consciously* creating them. Don't beat yourself up when you must change or break an agreement. Take responsibility and learn from your experience.

Research demonstrates that the practice of making and keeping agreements is directly related to life skills, such as an enhanced sense of healthy responsibility, greeting challenges as an opportunity for growth, and expanded flexibility and adaptability. Begin to practice consciously creating, changing, and breaking agreements. You will experience an enhanced efficiency and well-being, and your relationships will flourish.

Applying the Practice: Agreement

Step 1: Consciously create agreements. This will build trust with others.

Step 2: Consciously change and break agreements. Listen to all parties without judgment. Take responsibility for any consequences.

Step 3: Learn by noticing any patterns.

Step 4: Capture the power of no by doing the things you want to do.

CREDIT

1 Bradberry, T. (2014, August 18). 9 Things Successful People Won't Do. Retrieved from: https:// www.linkedin.com/today/post/article/20140818190427-50578967-9-things-successful-peo-ple-won-t-do

CHAPTER 18

CONSCIOUS APPRECIATION

Every living thing requires attention to grow. We love to feel connected to ourselves and others. When we feel connected, everything flows—especially at work. Our projects run smoothly and productively. Our ability to sustain this connection directly affects our ability to create a culture and atmosphere of positive energy. One very effective way of achieving this result is through appreciation.

The negativity bias in the world is strong, so strong that often we focus on what went wrong with a project, how we failed, and how we are making mistakes. It's important to learn from our mistakes of course, but we miss out on the moment-to-moment opportunities to appreciate others and our situations by overlooking what's going well—especially during conflict. It's time to expand our nervous systems and become fluent in the language of positive energy to capitalize on the power of connection. We can do this through appreciation.

In his *Harvard Business Review* blog, Tony Schwartz reveals, "The single highest driver of engagement, according to a worldwide study conducted by Towers Watson, is whether workers feel their managers are genuinely interested in their wellbeing. Less than forty percent of workers felt so engaged. Feeling genuinely appreciated lifts people up. At the most basic level, it makes us feel safe, which is what frees us to do our best work. It's also energizing."[1]

So why is it so difficult to run on positive energy and appreciation? Beyond the world's negativity bias, we are not skillful in giving and receiving positive energy, whether it be appreciating ourselves, others, or our current situations.

Consider these real client experiences: the senior executive who didn't feel appreciated by her firm and, when asked what would it take for her to feel appreciated, responded, "I don't know;" the team leader who has no regular practice of appreciation for his team and is wondering why morale has dropped; the engineer who avoids appreciation from others and can't figure out why she is so unhappy. Often, we have a cap on the amount of positive energy we will allow. Some people have difficulty accepting positive comments and appreciation. You'll know these individuals by watching their facial expressions or posture when you deliver some appreciation to them. They cringe, turn away, or ask, "What do you mean by that?"

We are confident in expressing our negative opinions about a person or situation, and we are often confident in accepting the negative things people say to us, whether it's true or not. Instead, we can expand our nervous systems, and become proficient in uplifting and expanding attention—the way of positivity. I am not talking about creating an environment where you and your colleagues walk around all day superficially cheer leading each other. There is a huge opportunity here to evolve beyond the negativity bias to give positive bias equal weight when appropriate.

To be masterful at appreciation is to genuinely and specifically acknowledge some nuance or characteristic. Most people express appreciation in the form of general platitudes such as *"Great job!"* or *"You are awesome."* As repeated appreciations, these become stale and fall on deaf ears. To be skillful is to be genuine, specific, and detailed. Consider the delivery of *"I appreciate how diligently you focused during our team meeting and kept the group on track,"* or *"I appreciate how you were empathetic with her while at the same time holding her accountable."* Think about how it would feel to receive that information versus, *"Good job with that,"* or *"That was well done."*

When you feel that you want to show appreciation to someone, take some breaths, focus on the details of what you want to express, and then speak. Once you have said what you've determined to share, stop talking and give the receiver a chance to accept your words.

Appreciation applies to you, too. Take time each day to appreciate something about yourself. You can ask yourself in the moment, *"What do I feel proud of right now?"* or *"What's going well for me now?"* The easiest way to cultivate positive energy with others is to begin with yourself.

Join me in an Appreciation Challenge. Try to outnumber your criticisms with appreciations by a ratio of five to one. Tony Schwartz said, "In the workplace itself, researcher Marcial Losada has found that among high-performing teams, the expression of positive feedback outweighs that of negative feedback by a ratio of 5.6 to 1. By contrast, low-performing teams have a ratio of .36 to 1."[1]

Go to www.abigailstason.com and download my bonus chapter and worksheet. They support what you have learned in this chapter.

Applying the Practice: Conscious Appreciation

Step 1: Commit to mindfully expanding your nervous system by giving and receiving appreciations.

Step 2: Start with the practice of giving five appreciations throughout your day—to yourself and others.

Step 3: See if you can increase your number from there. Remember, what you focus on expands, so the more you appreciate, the more you'll have to appreciate.

CREDIT ————————————————————————

1 T Schwartz. (2012, January 23). Why Appreciation Matters So Much. Retrieved from http:// blogs.hbr.org/2012/01/ why-appreciation-matters-so-mu/

CHAPTER 19

DON'T GOSSIP—CONNECT

Gossip is something we can all identify with, and it's one of the things I've found most troubling to deal with in corporate cultures, as well as in personal relationships. Let me take a step back and say that gossip used to be helpful. It was a way that groups cooperated and applied accountability. This is a long time ago, when laws, social structures, and standards didn't exist. It's time to evolve past gossip to communicate and hold people accountable. Don't beat around the bush. Gossip is toxic and separates us rather than bringing us closer.

When we gossip, we erode integrity and morale. Anxiety among employees increases as rumors circulate without any clear information as to what is fact and what is fiction. Relationships deteriorate based on the lack of clear communication and true information. Divisiveness grows as people take sides. The culture of a company becomes poisonous.

While all this is important, the most critical effect of gossip is that it erodes our brand, our self-esteem, and our connection with the truth of who we are.

Gossip is commonly used as a strategy to avoid a touch conversation, to mask an unconscious agenda, and to avoid any discomfort. I find that people gossip to avoid speaking directly to another person—to avoid a hard conversation. Consider these *real* statements between colleagues.

"Can you believe what he did the other day at the meeting?"

"I never trust her because she has the ear of the CEO."

"I saw the CEO and CFO talking, and I'll bet another round of layoffs is coming."

"I heard that he screwed up the presentation, and now the project isn't moving forward."

"What do you think of her? She talks too much."

Often, there is no clear guidance from leadership around gossip. I can remember being in meetings to discuss a staff member's performance. The unspoken intent of the conversation was not to facilitate growth and productivity, but rather to tear the person down. Rather than discussing the behavior and ways to champion the individual into their potential, the discussion focused on everything the individual was doing wrong.

I have two clients whose performance was part of a normal calibration process. Their two managers were talking about them to a third party, and this information got back to my clients. They heard about their performance from someone other than their manager through gossip!

As I walk around company campuses, I overhear people talking about other people in a way that is not compassionate. Consider this real dialog that I overheard while walking across the campus of a technology company.

Person 1: "He never finishes his part of the project. He never does."

Person 2: "No one wants to work with him."

Person 3: "Everyone hates him."

Person 1: "Yeah, everyone hates him."

Such dialog can make it very easy to start judging. As I overheard this exchange, I felt compassion for these three individuals and for the person they were gossiping about. They probably weren't aware of the impact and ripple affect they had.

My goal here is to inspire you to rise above this type of behavior and to do so I am providing you a better understanding of gossip and the process to make a more compassionate and connected choice with how to interact and share information.

Gossip

What is gossip? Does the person need to be absent for it to be gossip? Does there need to be a hidden agenda for it to be gossip? Does it have to be negative? Is saying good things about someone gossip? Is gossip a choice? The answer to all is *yes*. However, only you know if you are gossiping.

Here are some working definitions of gossip. According to Websters. com, "Gossip can be considered a rumor, a report of an intimate nature, chatty talk, the subject matter of gossip. A gossip is someone who habitually reveals personal or sensational facts about others."[1]

"Gossip is casual, unconstrained conversation or reports about other people, typically involving details that are not confirmed as being true."[2] It is "Idle talk or rumor about the personal or private affairs of others. It is one of the oldest and most common means of sharing facts and views, but also has a reputation for the introduction of errors and variations into the information transmitted. The term can also imply that the idle chat or rumor is of personal or trivial nature as opposed to normal conversation. Other experts identify gossip as: 'A form of workplace violence, noting it is essentially a form of attack; any language that would cause another harm, pain, or confusion that is used outside the presence of another for whom it is intended.'"[3]

In its simplest form, gossip is talking about someone who is not in the room, to fill some hidden agenda, avoid some interaction, or to fill a gap in experience.

The truth is that we *do* gossip about others. We talk about people all the time; the sharing of information can help to connect us and communicate. The question is, "When you are talking about someone who is not in the room, what is your intention behind it?" Is it to grow and develop this person and help them progress in any action regarding the project? Is it to increase or diminish my connection with the person I'm with? If the intention is to share information, to share knowledge, to move forward the progress on a project, or to learn about others, that can be helpful. But if you intend to tear someone down, to disconnect from someone, or to bring harm to a project, it is counterproductive.

Gossip Equals Drama

While gossip is expressed through our words, gossip is also a posture. What do I mean by gossip posture? It is a feeling in your body combined with your intention. When people are gossiping, they are typically filled with adrenaline and experience shortness of breath and muscle contraction. Your body sensations are as important, if not more important, than what you are saying.

If you share information or to champion a person, project or cause, you will not be in your gossip posture. Your breath will be easy, and you will be sharing information for forwarding an action, or for the benefit of others, for the greater good.

Typically, people have a gossip voice, pace, and tone. You may even have a phrase that you start with when you are gossiping such as, *"Did you hear about . . .?" "Boy, have I got a story for you," "Get a load of this one," "I have to tell you what he did yesterday."* When you gossip, you take your attention away from yourself to avoid your experience—usually to avoid feelings—and place it on someone else. You create drama. These combined sensations, tones, and interactions constitute your gossip posture. As you pay close attention to your posture and behavior, you will start to recognize a pattern when speaking about others.

This is one of the most powerful shifts for people and yet the most difficult. Like everything else in this book, it requires self-mastery. When you find yourself talking about someone else, stop and check it out. You will find there is another person to whom you want to speak or a conversation you are avoiding. Don't miss the opportunity to connect with someone.

Applying the Practice: Don't Gossip

Step 1: Notice when you are talking about someone else.

Step 2: Stop and notice your words, your gossip posture, and your intention.

Step 3: Bring your attention back to your own experience and be present.

Step 4: Share your own experience instead of talking about someone else.

CREDIT ————————————————————

1 http://dictionary.reference.com/browse/gossip?s=t

2 http://www.oxforddictionaries.com/us/definition/american_english/gossip

3 http://en.wikipedia.org/wiki/Gossip

CHAPTER 20

PAY ATTENTION—THRIVE CONSCIOUSLY

There is remarkable congruence between what we claim to stand for and how we live our lives. This is possible by getting clear about what's important to us. Knowing our values is a great place to start and helps us align our activities toward activities we enjoy. Aside from values, I find myself continually teaching people how to thrive. In the absence of conscious action around thriving, our unconscious habits will take over. Our routines will be on autopilot, and we experience the roller-coaster ups and downs of feeling energized or feeling exhausted. People struggle with work/life balance, and no wonder! They don't sit down and take stock in what allows them to thrive.

For instance, we outsource our health, unconsciously following "what has always been done." When we don't feel well, we go to the doctor and take a pill. We are so out of touch with our bodies that we don't realize they have huge capacity to heal us if we consciously choose to collaborate with them. We can be conscious of our health and take the time to become educated about what we put into our bodies. We can ask, *"Are we consuming food that is nutritious?"* We can be conscious about what we eat or drink, rather than staying on autopilot and numbing ourselves with food or alcohol. We can empower ourselves around our health instead of outsourcing it to doctors and corporations. We can change the healthcare landscape through our individual choices.

Money is a difficult subject for many people. Just as with other patterns, we have unconscious commitments about wealth and money. We can all choose to spend our money, as well as earn our money, in alignment with our values, hopefully considering the good of all. We can save our money without fear and share it with causes that are relevant to us, transferring our wealth to next generations free of entanglements, without imposing *our* values on our heirs. To to do this, we must act *consciously* when we allow old patterns to drive our financial behaviors. Essentially, we are voting with every dollar on how we want to treat each other and our planet.

To provide another way to practice, when I think of thriving I think of four core pillars of well-being: Physical, Mental, Emotional, and Spiritual. Since many people create stress about money, the fifth is an honorable mention—Financial.

Physical   Mental   Emotional   Spiritual   Financial

Figure 13

To live in balance, we must give attention to each of these four pillars. If we neglect any one, our life and our health will be out of balance. All four pillars are connected. Improving physical health helps our emotional health. Sound spiritual health will support us in mental health.

Physical health. Become a master of caring for your human body, attending carefully to sleep, exercise, and nutrition via whole foods. Know and honor the importance of rest, rhythms, integration, and renewal. Worship your body like a temple; anything you put into your body has an effect toward or away from thriving. Below are some specific factors to consider:

- **Sleep patterns.** Pay attention to the duration, quality, and consistency of your sleep.

- **Food and drink.** Incorporate plenty of water and organic fruits and vegetables, less sugar and processed foods, alcohol, caffeine, drugs, etc.

- **Exercise and movement.** Moving and physically exercising regularly, including the cardiovascular, increase your heart rate, which assists in toxin elimination through the lungs and sweat glands; beware of sitting too long or sitting with poor posture.

- **Relaxation or down time.** Include relaxation time to rest, recover, and integrate, incorporating relaxing activities such as taking naps, baths, etc.

- **Breathe.** Use slow abdominal, or belly breathing, which promotes good health; rapid, shallow chest breathing indicates stress.

- **Listen to your body.** Learn to listen to and not override the body's need for sleep, food, exercise, rest, etc.

- **Stress reduction.** Practice entering the healing state versus the stress state.

The physical health presencing question is, *"In this moment, are my choices aligned with physical burnout or thriving?"*

Mental health. Drop your mental stories and get real. Go beyond your ego so that the mind is a servant to being-ness, accessing wisdom and pure intelligence that is consciousness. Let go of your personal agenda and act for the good of all. Here are some specific factors to consider:

- **Positive and negative.** Consider the impact of positive and negative thinking and visualization on health and stress levels.

- **Focus on the present.** Focus thoughts on the task in the present moment versus ruminating about the past or worrying about the future.

- **Release the chatter.** Let go of the stories and mind chatter, even telling the truth. Capitalize on meditation if necessary.

- **Ignore the critic.** Ignore your inner critic and commit to high self-esteem.

- **Align with your values.** Become aligned with your values versus your familial and cultural conditioning.

The mental health presencing question is, *"In this moment, am I willing to listen to my deeper wisdom and let go of what my mind/ego thinks should happen?"*

Emotional health. Be a master of allowing feelings to flow and capture the wisdom from emotions. Conscious leaders know that emotions are just energy that comes and goes as phenomena. Overcoming fear is overcoming stress—boost your immune system with emotional flow. Some specific factors to consider are:

- **Emotional intelligence.** Identify emotions and their wisdom.

- **Mastering fear.** Study the four fear responses.

- **Presence versus The Drama Triangle.**

- **Emotions.** Express emotions constructively. Stay current with your emotions and give space to intense emotional experiences.

- **Connect.** Connect with yourself and others in meaningful ways, such as touch, time together, etc.

The emotional health presencing question is, *"How can I welcome my emotional energy and fully be in my experience?"*

Spiritual health. Open fully to allow life to flow through you and realize that *you are not in control.* Evolved beings have full access to spirit and source and are guided by something larger than themselves; know that personal growth is an endless journey, and everything is in service of awakening to the truth of who we are. Some specific factors to consider are:

- **Self-inquiry.** Who am I? Connect deeply with your true self and allow this to guide you instead of your thoughts.

- **Being versus doing.** Act from a place of presence versus staying busy out of fear.

- **Inner versus outer searching.** Look within for answers and fulfillment.

- **Identify.** Do not identify with anything that comes and goes; instigate vigilance to what is always here.

- **True nature.** Know that peace, freedom, and love are your true nature and birthright.

- **Disrupters.** Stopping, silence, and stillness are the ultimate disrupters.

The spiritual health presencing questions are, *"What does my life stand for? Who am I?"*

Financial health. Be a master of allowing your feelings to flow with regard to wealth, and understand triggers and stressors. Remember that money is a necessary part of the structure of exchange, and true wealth comes from inner peace and freedom. Take responsibility for wealth management by understanding finances as well as the capacity for risk. Some factors to consider are:

- **Values.** Know your values and those activities that bring you satisfaction and fulfillment.

- **Spending and investment.** Spend and invest your wealth in alignment with your values versus subscribing to the *keeping up with the Jones' syndrome.*

- **Plan.** Plan for saving and accumulating wealth.

- **Share.** Share philanthropically in those causes that you are passionate about versus just writing a check.

- **Bequeath.** Transfer your wealth to heirs with no strings attached, to honor their values.

The financial health presencing question is, *"Do I believe that having wealth is good for humanity and the planet?"* If the answer is *no,* refer to the first four pillars.

These four-plus-one pillars are a framework for you to inventory your well-being. Use this at any time. I recommend reviewing it every six months. Well-being is an ongoing process, and you must stay conscious to be attuned to the cycles of life. It's okay if during a cycle you are not thriving; however, it is imperative that you are *consciously* choosing not to adjust. It's very easy for unconscious patterns to emerge that will put you back on the hamster wheel—the road to burnout. You can't be an effective, conscious leader if you are exhausted, burnt out, and unhappy. When we thrive as individuals, we can be more resilient leaders, our teams will thrive, as will our organization.

For your conscious thriving practice, go to www.abigailstason.com and download my worksheets.

CHAPTER 21

THE IMPORTANCE OF INTEGRATION

Integration is a critical process to bring into conscious awareness. It is where we consciously allow parts, pieces, elements, and moments of our experiences to be combined into the whole of our humanity and consciousness. While we are unconsciously engaging in this process all day long, I invite you to make it more proactive and deliberate, for at times this requires us to stop taking in new data and allow our brain and body to settle in. In the absence of conscious integration, we usually create some unconscious version of activity to force ourselves to stop.

We have a limited capacity to take in information, but an unlimited ability to store information. When we flood our nervous systems, we end up discovering *we do have a limit* as to what we can absorb at that moment. Our nervous system strives for homeostasis and has limits to the level of negative and positive experiences it can handle. We can even become overloaded *positive* experiences. This is one of our most obvious opportunities, expanding into positive energy for extended periods of time, rather than sabotaging ourselves waiting for the bomb to drop when things are going so well. In all our experiences, we eventually reach our maximum limit and end up topping out if we do not integrate.

In a world of *doing*, overloading our nervous system is on the top of the list revealing how we keep ourselves from being in a constant state of flow. Here are some common symptoms of overloading the nervous system:

- Finding fault with yourself or others
- Looking for what's wrong
- An increase of worry about the future or the past
- Irritability with family, colleagues, or general irritability
- Becoming ill
- Starting an argument with someone
- Creating different types of drama in our interactions
- Self-deprecating thoughts
- Losing attention at meetings
- Acting out
- Feeling tired and sleepy
- Overeating to feel better
- Tripping, falling, or general clumsiness
- In severe cases, getting in accidents

Of all of these, the most common example is an illness. Our bodies know when it's time to stop and integrate. As achievers, we push our limits. Without conscious integration, our bodies will create conditions for us to stop and we can become physically unwell.

Are you getting enough sleep? Our bodies integrate automatically every night through sleep. When we sleep, our bodies perform a series of processes: blood pressure drops and muscles relax, tissue growth and repair is initiated, energy is restored, hormones are released. Sleep provides energy to the brain and body for daytime performance.

Research shows that most of us need seven or eight hours of sleep every night. Studies show that prolonged sleep deprivation is the same as being under the influence of alcohol. For this reason, you must be conscious of your circadian rhythm. Stemming from your hypothalamus, your circadian rhythm is your internal clock that is your asleep/awake cycle. Your circadian rhythm is sensitive to daylight and dark. When it starts to become night, your hypothalamus sends signals for your body to release melatonin and you begin to feel tired. Therefore, it's difficult to function without a regular sleep cycle around the same time of day.

What's exciting is the wave of new science available to us regarding the importance of sleep. I cannot stress enough that if you think you can function without the appropriate amount of sleep required by your nervous system, you are kidding yourself.

Your brain needs to rest. Research shows that the brain needs to rest from concentrated focus. Be conscious of your ultradian rhythm. To not overwork any part of your brain, you will experience a natural lull in your concentration. This is your natural ultradian rhythm in action. This rhythm is sensitive to brain-wave frequencies. In short, your brain needs a break every ninety to one-hundred-twenty minutes. When you are utilizing concentrated brain activity, without enough rest, it can be impossible to power through and stay focused.

While writing *Evolution Revolution,* I set a timer for no more than ninety minutes. When I heard the buzzer, I stopped writing and took at least a fifteen-minute break, even if I didn't feel I needed it. Instead of powering through the natural mental lull, I stopped. By honoring my ultradian rhythms, I am sharper when I *do* write. I make *more* progress in *less* time. Writing feels less like work and more like creative flow. These *brain timeouts* are worth their weight in gold and counterintuitive to every pressure in our society.

Bring integration into your day-to-day. You can integrate during the day and not just when sleeping. Conscious integration is a practice where you give your brain and whole body a chance to take in the entirety of your experiences. It is necessary for experiences and information to go into the data bank of your subconscious so it can be called forward later. By proactively integrating throughout your day, you allow your nervous system to renew itself so that you can take on more.

Your body is already doing this moment-by-moment. For instance, with regard to emotions, when feelings are not repressed, we experience them directly. The energy flows through our nervous system organically. The experience is integrated into our entire body and being so we can capture any wisdom or pure intelligence when appropriate. Most times, the experience of emotion is integrated fully with nothing to do other than to allow it to settle into our subconscious. This is an integrated experience.

One of the ways we disintegrate our experience is by repressing our emotions. We disown our feelings and our experience. The experience of feelings will not be integrated into the whole of our bodies and be-ings. The energy it takes to split off these experiences is a huge drain on the nervous system. We block the natural integrative process and become tired.

Be more conscious. Using the example of emotions helps us to see our propensity to avoid emotions. This applies to any experience. Honoring our integrative processes is easier said than done. We say: *"I can't stop in the middle of a meeting," "My kids need to get to soccer," "I have to get this project done," "I don't have time to stop, meditate, or rest," "I have too much to do."*

We must acknowledge we *do* have agreements to keep, activities to up-hold in our lives, and we want to make an impact; but we also need to acknowledge the challenges of parenting and other such circumstances that we experience where it's not easy to get enough rest or sleep. We *may* con-sciously choose to overload our nervous systems; but when we are conscious of our actions, we are able to make choices in favor of ourselves. Determine what the cost will be to us and others for not paying attention to ourselves.

What Does Integration Look Like in Practice?

Integration processes vary for each person. First we must recognize the symptom that indicates our nervous system is overloaded. We will feel full—mentally, physically, emotionally, even spiritually

Figure 14

After recognizing we have reached our capacity, it's time to integrate. Become skillful with integrative practices. One basic integration practice is to stop, be still, and rest. In doing so, our minds are stopped, and we are not creating new experiences, taking in new information. Here is how I integrate:

- **Be in nature.** Don't hike while integrating. Walk slowly or sit. Don't choose a new trail as that might require too much focus.

- **Meditation and ambient music.** Integrate by donning some headphones and listen to ambient music that has been scientifically proven to reduce anxiety.

- **Rest.** Lie down, and allow our bodies to rest and restore.

- **Presencing.** Use the presencing process to be sure we are current with our experience.

- **Feel any unfelt emotions.** Open to any unfelt emotions for the day. When current with our emotions, we are integrated human beings.

- **Television.** Watch TV, but watching something we've already seen so we don't have to think about it, and it will be more of an ambient background noise.

- **Retreats.** Attend a couple retreats every year and rest and restore ourselves. This usually includes healthy food, some easy movement, meditation, massages, and anything else that supports the nervous system.

- **Oxygen.** An excellent support for the nervous system is oxygen. Just breathe.

Any of these activities can be taxing to your nervous system and, therefore, not true integration. Don't lie down and turn on the television, or be on your laptop where focused attention is required. A retreat where you are learning something *new* is not integration. These activities require our attention as we have not experienced them before—which contradicts the benefits of integration whose entire point is to renew.

I hesitated mentioning television because it can be a trap, as can social media. Integration is an *active* process, not an *escape*. When we escape, we are not engaged in life. It can be useful to mentally check out, but this is *not* integration. Consider these ideas:

- **Activities.** Do you like to move when integrating? Some people get the most out of integrating while running, cycling, or some other form of easy activity. Any movement for integration should not push your physical limits.

- **Silence and stillness.** Is it easier to integrate when we are silent and still? Some people find it easier to rest in an atmosphere of total calm.

- **Add movement.** For some, the best experience for integrating includes a mixture of movement and stillness. For me, Qigong is an integrative practice. During Qigong, I am moving very slowly, and my mind is still.

- **Nourish and rest.** What do you find nourishing and restful? Some people like to listen to music, dance, or have a cup of tea. Others like to journal or draw.

How we integrate will be unique to each of us. Focusing on something that allows our minds and bodies the space to renew is the goal. Avoid taking in new information. Find a way to achieve calming thoughts, so the new information is in the background, and our heartbeat, or breathing, comes to the forefront. As we experiment, we will discover we are already aware of techniques that are very familiar to us. Any successful techniques should increase energy and enhance vitality after we've integrated.

Real Examples

A few years back, my father passed away. Lewy Body Dementia, the same disease that took Robin Williams' life, took my dad. He lived on the east coast. I live in California. Near the end of his life, I flew across the country quite frequently to be with him. During the last few months of his life, there were some financial and other affairs to put in order. Visiting with him was a gift, and I never knew when it would be our last conversation. I felt angry, scared, and sad as the dementia affected him and his ability to recognize me. Life consisted of visits to see him, coordinating his financial affairs, as well as researching some short-term care for him that included transporting him back to the northeast for long-term care. (My family is from New Jersey.)

When I say that this experience was huge, I can't even describe how overwhelmed I felt *every* day. I didn't feel like a victim. I simply knew that my nervous system could handle only so much, and on the top of the list was the death of my father.

I tried my best to integrate. I told my colleagues that I wasn't available for work. While I was out of the office, I didn't check my email. I explained that I had enough to deal with. Every night I tried to catch up on my experience by presencing my emotions and experience. I tried to keep up my healthy diet and get out for a short walk every day. I did the best that I could under very stressful circumstances. I share this story to acknowledge that the practice of integration is easier said than done, especially when life presents some severe challenges. Also, I share it because when we are *not* so challenged, there is no excuse for integrating.

Your Team Will Be Stronger When You Integrate

Bringing it back to the workplace, I coached a team leader from a technology company. The team was on lock-down for a month preparing for a product launch. (Lock-down is where a team becomes super focused on only the project—limiting meetings and extraneous activities, etc.) The team was in the last phase of the project. Many coordinated action steps were being prepared and much code needed to be written and finalized. Pre-launch is an intense time. No one made space to integrate. The members of the team hit their limit and, instead of recognizing it, they started to find fault in their product. Creating a swirl of activity to try to feel better, they proposed that the project abruptly change directions, an unreasonable discussion given the status of the project and impending launch date. A week was wasted as team members argued and created drama.

I saw my client, the leader of the team, on a Thursday afternoon, the same week the team was in drama. I suggested to the leader that he instruct everyone to take the weekend off, to rest and relax over the weekend rather than continue to work on the project. To him, this was ridiculous. He said, "We are about to launch. There's no way we cannot work this weekend." I pointed out that the team was tired, in drama, and not being productive. I challenged him to try something new to create a different outcome. He took a chance and told the team to take the weekend off.

On Monday morning, having had the weekend to relax and integrate their experience, the team understood because of the new ideas that were presented, the new direction would leave them more work to do. They also realized they were right on target and nothing had to be changed. By having permission to rest, restore, and integrate, they became refocused, and the launch was successfully completed. For your business, consider what the loss of income would be with days of no productivity, but in the end, a result that could create faster productivity because of the time the team had to ruminate over the new direction.

Individual Examples

- The movie or rock stars who ascend so quickly they are over their heads, can't adapt, and end up blowing up their reputation with immature behavior
- The fiancés who pick fights with each other because they are overwhelmed by all of the experiences of the wedding
- The multiple technology company employees who burn out because they don't make space to integrate
- The senior executive who moves from activity to activity and who is so tired, his marriage is struggling
- The company whose work/life balance internal survey scores are low although they advocate for thriving
- The engineer who puts such strong pressure on himself to perform he refuses to take a break and becomes short-tempered
- The newly promoted executive who diminishes his presence by not consciously realizing his steep learning curve, and he can't keep up

Integration is necessary to support the nervous system to carry out what we desire to do in the world. We do ourselves and others a disservice if we honor our natural rhythms. We will make a bigger impact in the world as we learn to take relentless care of ourselves.

Applying the Practice: Integration—Let Your Nervous System Rest

Step 1: Be aware of when you start to exceed your capacity for experiences. Consciously choose to integrate as soon as you can.

Step 2: Experiment how to integrate proactively and support your nervous system.

Step 3: When working on a team or in an organization, encourage the space for yourself and others to proactively integrate.

Step 4: Take inventory of your circadian and ultradian rhythms, and start to implement small changes.

Step 5: Don't just go through the motions—integrate!

CHAPTER 22

WHAT'S NEXT?

You've just read a series of practices that will raise your consciousness—you will be more evolved. By being masterful, you clear away static and re-channel time and energy toward leading others and leading a more fulfilling life.

The practices here are specifically designed for use in your day-to-day. You may already embrace conscious leadership. What I intend here is to bridge Eastern and Western practices by putting consciousness into action in your moment-to-moment activities. It's not enough to talk about consciousness; you must immerse yourself in these skills to evolve. As Einstein said, "You cannot solve a problem in the same level of consciousness that created it."

Many of these tools are simple and seem obvious. The truth is that they are simple and powerful. However, what is required of you is to implement them for transformation and evolution to occur.

You are probably noticing how I am using the words skills, tools, and practices. I want to stress that they are just that, *practices*. You must practice! Like building any muscle, you will need to exercise and retrain your nervous system to overcome autopilot conditioning. Perfection is not required. In fact, I highly discourage the quest for or expectation of perfection. What you are seeking is awareness. The skills will raise your awareness, granting you access to more profound and more authentic insights. Practice doesn't make you perfect; it makes you conscious and evolved.

It is your choice where you focus your attention. Your progress can be measured by noticing how quickly you are closing the gap in time between your old unconscious behavior and your new evolved way of being.

As you can probably see, these skills are not for the faint of heart. The question is, are you willing to overcome conditioning and old ways of being that are no longer of service? In an information age, everything is changing. What is required of all of us? Conscious interactions, agility, compassion, evolution—all are necessary. Not everyone will be available for this challenge. For me, I am willing regardless of others. You will notice a change in your relationships—be prepared. When people are stuck in unconscious patterns, they aren't always able to see this, and they may not be willing to learn. As you wake up and evolve, human dynamics will change.

Finally, I want to point out that the context for this book is leadership. These practices obviously apply everywhere, in all relationships, in parenting, in friendships, and across cultures. We are not finished yet.

PART TWO

Unconscious Bias and Stereotyping

CHAPTER 23

WAKE UP AND JOIN THE CONVERSATION

With social media and technology providing access to information, and we now see how divided we are as a country, society, and species. There's no global conversation that's more timely, relevant, and important than that of bias, stereotyping, and prejudice. The date is August 16, 2017. Just last week, a group of white supremacists descended on the city of Charlottesville, Virginia, claiming to be defending the legacy of the Confederacy. Counter-protesters met the group, clashes broke out, and police started to disperse the crowds. The gathering became violent, resulting in the death of one person and the injury of thirty more. Some of the white supremacists were carrying Nazi flags and chanting, "Jews will not replace us!" It is clear on the video that they were chanting the last four words. However, it's difficult to absolutely say that the first word was "Jews." It could have been "You." The last four words were the essential message.

This very violent exchange sparked endless discussions on social media, much of it blaming, shaming, condemning. In fact, much of the news over the last two years here in the United States and around the globe has been filled with discussions about our divisiveness as a human species. One of the benefits and drawbacks of technology and social media—it has brought to light the horrors of this divisiveness. We cannot change something if we are not willing to see it, social media shows us how harmfully we treat each other, and we are forced to confront these horrors.

We are at a crossroads, and we've been here before. What's different now versus the past is the amount of information available to us, the advances in science, and an open global world offered to us due to technology. Here lies an opportunity to meet the evolutionary offering presented to us to evolve past conditioning, through conscious accelerated growth and learning. We can start to embrace our fellow humans, learn about each other, and close the gap of divisiveness. We can understand why we act the way we do and, with compassion and boundaries, learn new ways of behaving and respond peacefully.

The topic of stereotyping is so critical. And this is another invitation to wake up and come out of the trance of conditioning, to become more conscious and make choices in favor of humanity and the planet.

There is a plethora of information about the benefits of diversity. Clearly, diversity and inclusion provide new ideas, appreciation for different cultural backgrounds, potential for learning, more collaboration among teams, and a market advantage. Despite these benefits, we continue to exclude others. Even with laws against segregation, there is still much divisiveness in the United States, as well as across the globe.

There are laws, processes, and systems in place to prevent discrimination. Obviously, these are useful. To continue to review and rewrite such programs is also useful. No matter the laws in place, it is people who enforce or don't enforce them. If we are not aware of how we discriminate as individuals, no process will be effective.

That's not to say there is a simple solution to these very challenging and complex problems that exist regarding discrimination; however, we can each do our part by learning how we contribute to the problem. From there, we can begin to be part of the solution. While I do advise companies on how to overcome bias in their organizations, the focus is now on you as an individual and what you can do. Because I am so passionate about this topic, I am going to walk you through my own experience of stereotyping and bias and, specifically, the action steps I am taking to make sure I am inclusive. First, create a picture of me based on the following information:

I was born in 1966 and grew up in New Jersey. Now, does your impression of me change when I tell you that it was a very small town in New Jersey? A town surrounded by farmland, not like Newark, New Jersey? In high school, I played basketball and field hockey. I graduated and attended a small liberal arts college in Pennsylvania. My major was finance. When I graduated from college, I became the Chief Operating Officer of a tiny bank in my hometown. After three years, I left the bank and went to work on Wall Street. I worked my way up the ladder to sales leadership. For a time, I worked in lower Manhattan. After a nineteen-year career, I left and became a consciousness facilitator. I've lived in the Bay Area now for over ten years.

By now, you think you are aware that you have enough information about me to make informed decisions, that you could probably guess what I like and don't like, what kind of experience I have, and my expertise. You probably have a vision in your head of what I look like even though I haven't shared my race. I am white and female, by the way. I invited you to create a mental image of me because it's *what we do all the time!* We make a vision in our mind of the other person. If I hadn't mentioned it, you would have done it anyway. Realize that we create impressions of each other automatically.

My hometown was 100 percent white. I recognized this early in my childhood. Knowing this would limit my possibilities for growth, it was inevitable that I would eventually leave for a more diverse area. There is no denying that I come from a non-diverse, privileged background.

Now you have a better picture of me, Abby, let's go to the next chapter which contains my process to be more inclusive, to see others as me, so that I no longer make decisions influenced by my stereotyping. Finally, when it comes to topic, being awake to ourselves in how we relate in the world is critical. To overcome the suffering that we are separate from one another, a commitment to lifelong learning and evolution is necessary. This is just another opportunity to be conscious and contribute in the world in a way that invites a more peaceful existence.

CHAPTER 24

WHAT ARE WE TALKING ABOUT EXACTLY?

I t's not enough to talk about inclusion. If we want to be inclusive, we must *want and commit* to inclusion. I grew tired of all the blaming and shaming about race and gender discrimination. Discrimination is such an important and complex issue that we can no longer waste time in severe drama trying to figure out who is to blame—we can take responsibility by moving forward. Immediately, I recognized that for me to be more inclusive, I must educate myself. Entire books had to be written and documentaries produced about this topic. Read and watch them. The reading and research I've done, along with my own leadership experience, has shown me it comes down again to consciousness—raising awareness. Being inclusive takes time, energy, and effort. For me to educate myself, I started with a very basic question. "What are we talking about exactly?"

We all have biases, and we all stereotype. It's part of the human condition. Here is the definition of stereotype: "A standardized mental picture that is held in common by members of a group and that represents an oversimplified opinion, prejudiced attitude, or uncritical judgment."[1] This is what our brain does. It thinks in stereotypes. This is necessary for ordinary living and functioning. Our brain categorizes everything and uses the categorization as the basis for normal prejudgment. No one is exempt from this process. In fact, if our brains did not categorize, we would not be able to function. Here is how we are programmed.

- We see someone.

- Our brain assigns them to a group. We categorize them.

- Then we assign the behaviors of that group to the individual.

- We stereotype them as part of that group and expect they will act in alignment with those behaviors. We create a personal and sometimes unreasonable judgment, bias or an implicit association about one.

- When they act in accordance with our bias, we are comfortable. When they don't, we are uncomfortable.

Stereotyping is very useful. It allows us to make a mental image of someone and to move quickly to act in ordinary living. The brain is wired for efficiency, not connection, and if it didn't categorize, we could not function. Sadly, three of the main attributes the brain seeks for categorization are race, gender, and age. People recognize faces from their own ethnic group more easily than other ethnic groups. Therefore, where stereotyping is harmful is in connecting with others or interacting with others via preconceived judgments and biases. Unfortunately, these biases, which can be negative, become harmful when we are making decisions about people: hiring, firing, promotions, allocation of resources, whether to give someone a loan, where we live, who our friends are and who we vote for.

We not only stereotype, but we also want to be around others from our preferred group, our "in group." We are not born to hate. We *are* born to survive, and one survival mechanism is stereotyping. When we stereotype as described above, we are seeking the answer to, "Are they part of *my* group or not?" If they are, we feel safe. If they are not, they are dangerous. We have a strong tendency to favor and prefer members of our "in group." Furthermore, research shows fear occurs faster in other race faces and that the amygdala associates something bad with them. The following dynamic immediately invites survival mode.

Me belongs to the group *Us*—Then It's *Us* Versus *Them*

The "in group" pressure to conform is very real. We are social animals and want connection. We love to be part of a group. This is useful and helpful. A drawback is it may cause us to feel our group is superior and, therefore, will survive. When we come from a place of survival with a "don't rock the boat, or you will be kicked out" mentality, bias will spread like wildfire and create a dynamic called stereotype threat. In his book, *Whistling Vivaldi,* Claude Steele writes, "These people know their group identity. They know how their society views it. They know they are doing something for which that view is relevant. They know, at some level, that they are in a predicament; their performance could confirm a bad view of their group and themselves, as members of the group. Over the years, we used several working names for this predicament—stigmatization, stigma pressure, stigma vulnerability, stereotype vulnerability. We settled on stereotype threat. This term captured the idea of a situational predicament as a contingency of their group identity, a real threat of judgment or treatment in the person's environment that went beyond any limitations within."[2]

There are many facets for which we stereotype—race, gender, age, culture, weight, religion, occupation, sexuality, socioeconomic status, and politics, to name a few. Some common stereotypes (implicit associations) that exist in the United States are:

- An association of white with being American and black with being harmful
- An association of male with career and female with family
- An association of male with science/math and female with arts
- As association of Asians with being good at math and not good leaders; Google "Asian jokes" to see all the stereotypes about Asian people
- A positive correlation between success and likability in men, a negative correlation between success and likability for women; as women are more successful, we become uncomfortable

Unfortunately, when left uninvestigated, these biases dictate and influence our activities. Does it need to be argued how the white equals American and the black equals harmful bias has affected every aspect of our country? We claim that we don't discriminate in this country. It is no longer politically correct to show prejudices, so progress has been made. However, we've fallen into the trap of impression management. Outwardly, we may not appear to discriminate, while inwardly the stereotyping is still in play, and we discriminate against black people and other people of color.

We can easily see and read about the repercussions from stereotypes regarding women in the workforce, especially regarding the family stereotype, but with this bias running consciously or unconsciously for years, there still is a pay gap between men and women. Women are expected to take care of the home when they have children *and* manage a career. There is a reignited women's movement about equality for women. Think about this—before1970, women could not keep a job if they were pregnant, could not run the Boston Marathon, nor get a credit card or open a bank account. They could not practice law, breastfeed in public, refuse to have sex with their husband, serve on a jury, or attend Harvard or Yale. This is a very real "glass ceiling" that existed for women, and some of it still exists today. There is a movement now to encourage young women to enroll in more science and math classes.

Real action is birthed from these stereotypes. Women and minorities are judged: (1) on proven accomplishments, where white men are judged on expected potential; (2) to have gotten lucky, where white men are judged to be naturally talented; (3) that there is a negative correlation between success and likability and a positive one for men. In short, we don't like seeing women succeed and be in roles of power—it's not aligned with the stereotype of female and family/arts. Along these lines, we even publicly shame women and men differently on social media. For women, we shame by threatening physical violence and rape. For men, we publicly shame them by threatening to get them fired from their jobs.

Stereotypes are self-fulfilling, and stereotype threat causes stress—a *real* physiological event occurs which impairs performance and cognition. We feel anxious because fear takes hold and all of the physiological symptoms of fear appear in our bodies. We are so busy allocating nervous system resources to social identity that our performance drops. Our mind will race with thoughts such as analyzing for or against the stereotype, feeling victimized, becoming heroes ourselves to "get over it," villainizing anyone for stereotyping, and questioning our self-esteem. Cognitive ability is used inefficiently when stereotype threat is in play.

This all seems almost ridiculous. Unfortunately, it's very real. Earlier this year, a white male friend said to me, "You shop like a guy." He was stereotyping me on the spot: female equals "like to shop." I can't stand shopping! I brought this to his attention, and he was shocked at how powerfully these implicit associations function.

At another time, I was with someone else, a founder of a startup. He is a white male. During a discussion, he mentioned, "Men make better engineers." Speaking of engineers, two of my clients have difficulty getting their voices heard by designers. They were stereotyped by the designers as too analytical. Finally, I am female and spent twenty years on Wall Street. I was always aware of stereotype-threat and the very real drain on my overall nervous system.

It's easy to get defensive and start judging yourself or others. You may even be judging me. Remember, this computation by the brain happens subconsciously; but it happens automatically. It's not personal. If you are like me, you insist that you don't discriminate. This is our opportunity to evolve, to make new implicit associations, to be aware of our wiring and adjust. It's another way we can wake up out of the trance of conditioning.

In his book, *So You've Been Publicly Shamed,* Jon Ronson refers to an email conversation with his friend, Adam Curtis, a documentary film maker: "They're turning social media into a giant echo chamber where what we believe is consistently reinforced by people who believe the same thing. The tech Utopians present this as a new kind of democracy. It isn't. It's the opposite. It locks people off in the world they started with and prevents them from finding out anything different. They get trapped in the system of feedback reinforcement. Twitter® passes lots of information around. But it tends to be the kind of information that people know that others in their group will like. What you get is a kind of mutual grooming. One person sends on information that they know others will respond to in accepted ways. And then, in return, those others will like the person who gave them that piece of information. Information becomes a currency through which you buy friends and become accepted into the system. That makes it very difficult for bits of information that challenge the accepted views to get in. They tend to get squeezed out. When someone says something that disturbs the agreed protocols of the system, the other parts react furiously and try to eject that destabilizing fragment and regain stability. And so the idea that there is another world of other people that have other ideas is marginalized in our lives."[3]

A revolution of evolution will not let this happen. We are all connected and, at the same time, remain in a bubble. It's time to connect beyond our differences and come together, even when we are very different and disagree.

CHAPTER 25

RECOGNIZE OUR OWN BIAS AND THE WIRING OF OUR BRAINS

Transformation and change begin with awareness and acceptance. Given all the information about how our brain works regarding race, gender, etc., I took the following action steps to learn about and come into harmony with how my brain works.

- I took the online test offered by Project Implicit called the Implicit Association Test–IAT (https://implicit.harvard.edu/implicit/). I highly recommend it. It was no surprise at all, based on my background, that my preferences fall into the typical stereotypes listed above. Learning this about myself was extremely disappointing. At the same time, with all the science and research currently available, there is a huge opportunity for us to evolve. I have embraced conscious evolution.

- I pay close attention to notice my responses around people who may be different. Looking for the "friend or foe" filter, I switch it to "automatic friend mode." Notice my reactions rather than implementing solutions. The more I learn about my nervous system, the better off I am.

- I recognize that uncomfortable feeling around people who are different, and I am very familiar with my fear patterns and when I am in survival mode.

- I refuse to stay tone deaf by accepting the fact that we do over 80 percent of our thinking in our subconscious mind. This is where implicit bias is working.

- I completed the Anti-Defamation League's Personal Self-Assessment of Anti-Bias Behavior.

The points above raised my awareness about my own biases. In raising *your* awareness, be kind and compassionate with yourself. It's not easy to recognize that you discriminate. I can remember feeling very angry at my IAT results, so much so that I began questioning the methodology. Remember that real change comes from facing and accepting. We must learn about our tendencies to be able to act differently.

CHAPTER 26

NAVIGATING BIAS DAY-TO-DAY

I f you are feeling uncomfortable about this topic, I am right there with you. It's normal and expected. Be aware that even while writing this book, my biases are influencing how and what I write. There is a lot of work to be done by all of us all to overcome inequality.

Here are some actions you may implement in your life. Because stereotyping and bias is such a significant part of our society, it is unreasonable to expect that we can change this overnight. Will we be able to overcome our biases? Maybe not; however, we can understand them and how they impact our relationships. This is our opportunity to evolve with an open global forum now. We must train our brains to *be* more open and global. In doing so, our behaviors will follow. We must invest time, energy, and effort for this paradigm to change.

It all begins with conscious commitment. We don't get what we want; we get what are committed to. In the absence of conscious commitments, our unconscious patterns will rule us. Nowhere is this more evident than in our stereotyping and bias. As much as everyone says they are committed to diversity and inclusion, the result shows what we are committed to. With regard to bias and stereotyping, there is more to "unlearn" than learn, and it is a *life-long process*. As a white female, when I look up and see myself surrounded by white people, I am not committed to diversity, even though I say I am. Years ago, this was true for me; my commitment was to my "in group" of white people. My current commitment is *to learn everything I can about my tendencies to stereotype, discriminate, exclude others, and how I allow my unconscious biases to influence me.* By stepping into this commitment, my conscious and unconscious awareness is brought top of mind. More action is necessary, but without a conscious commitment, it's like sailing without a rudder.

Be emotionally intelligent and feel your feelings about bias. Be more at ease with your experience as you presence any feelings about diversity and inclusion. These are tough interactions, conversations, and experiences. We must presence our emotions and experiences as we learn how we discriminate. To be discriminated against is already hard enough without repressing our emotions. Make sure to be current with your emotions.

Make the conscious effort to get to know people who are different than you. Join a new group, meet new people, especially people of a different race or different background. This doesn't mean you need to drop current networking or friendship circles. Simply, for every new white person I network with or befriend, I consciously make sure there is one of a different background. What comes to mind here is how our Speaker of the House, a white male, was severely shamed on social media because a picture he posted with his team showed how he surrounds himself with white people. Upon seeing it, the question I asked myself was, "Who is in *my* picture, and if a picture of me were taken with my friends and colleagues, would diversity come through?"

Consciously and with great effort, make new implicit associations. Stereotyping is a natural process of the brain; it's easy. What is *very difficult* is overriding bias. I recommended earlier that you take the Implicit Association Test and any other bias inventories.

- When we know our results, we can make new mental associations.

- Aside from our test results, now that we are more educated, we can recognize other stereotypes and make new mental associations for these.

Earlier I shared my IAT Test results. To remind you, I score with a preference for light skin tone. One day I went to a UPS Store to fax something. When I walked in the door, there were two black men behind the counter. My first thought was, *They can't be in charge here.* I caught myself in the moment. There it was! My bias for white people. At that moment, I made strong eye contact with them, smiled, and thought of a positive association. I started the mantra in my mind, *Black people are good, black people are good, black people are good.* I repeated this over and over and felt myself making this new association. I pay attention in my interactions for these types of reactions.

While watching television, I do the same. I am deliberate about what I watch on TV and the Internet. Studies show that implicit associations can be weakened with relatively minimal interventions. For me, it's working. I am noticing that I feel at ease around anyone who is different than me. I am not under any illusion that I have "cured myself," however, I do notice a difference in my interactions.

Master your practice of presence specifically in your decision-making. I am inviting everyone to "micromanage" ourselves. As exhausting as this might be, we must investigate until discernment becomes ingrained. Imagine if each of us reallocated just 10 percent of our time, energy, and effort to inclusion! I have asked, and continue to ask myself, all the following:

- When giving feedback are we fair and equitable? Typically, if someone is a stereotype we like, we will give more positive feedback. If someone is a stereotype we don't like, we will give more negative feedback or no feedback at all.

- Are we deciding in favor of your "in group?" That is, do we allocate more resources, time, and energy to our "in group?"

- Do we vote for diversity with the dollars we spend?

- For our philanthropic endeavors, do we make financial contributions to, or volunteer for, organizations that are for diversity? Favoritism through unconscious bias harms others even when it appears to be an altruistic action.

- Do we use our connections to help people who are just like us?

- Do we make any unconscious decisions that continue to divide people by money, social class, profession or any other quality that keeps the division in place?

- Do we bring into our awareness that our brain will stereotype and, therefore, affect any decision we make?

- Do we find ourselves labeling anyone, at any time?

- Do we accept and understand that we all stereotype? Do we ask the question, "Is my stereotype of someone else worthy of investigation, given my context?"

Catch yourself using labels. Very simply, try to avoid using labels with regard to people. By avoiding labels, we will be invited to get to know someone at a deeper level.

Don't sweep it under the carpet. Respond! It's important not to sweep bigoted and exclusive comments under the carpet. When someone uses bigoted language, racial jokes, and slurs, don't attack. But speak up! By doing so, we hold ourselves and others accountable.

Change our environment. Change what we see and are exposed to in our environment and what is reinforced through repeated exposure. Here mass media repeatedly exposes us to stereotyping, and it can also provide some counter-stereotypes. What is our environment, and do we make conscious choices to be in an environment that exposes us to diversity and inclusion?

Question employers and our own leadership. The demand is on ourselves and our employer to commit to diversity through direct programs, processes, and ongoing specific education. It's easy to sit back and criticize ourselves or our employer. Instead, keep demanding that diversity and inclusion be at the top of business and development goals.

Don't shame or blame ourselves or others. It's very easy to blame and shame others for how they treat people of a different race or gender. This is a waste of time and is toxic. Given that we all stereotype as a function, when we criticize someone, it's as if we are criticizing them for breathing. By blaming and shaming people through stereotyping them as alt-right, alt-left, white supremacists, neo-Nazis, etc., we add to the stereotyping. We can be more sophisticated by being specific and clear about what we do stand for: equality, respect, education, and peace. When we make blanket statements about a person who hates rather than label them and shame them as "bad," we can point out respectfully how their actions harm others and promote inequality. I don't mean to oversimplify here, and this is much easier said than done, but blaming and shaming get us nowhere.

Spark real discussions about diversity in all our interactions. Instead of the blame/shame game, we can spark some honest and real discussions about stereotyping. When we create a forum for real conversations, people feel safe to talk about their stereotypes, for when we accept ourselves, then real change can happen. In all my circles, we consciously discuss discrimination, how we add to it, and how we can overcome it. And when someone puts their foot in their mouth, we consider it a good thing, because we've raised awareness and can make a new choice. Ideally, if we can to get to a place where anyone can admit to, and speak to their biases without being attacked, then we've made real progress.

Surround ourselves with people who are committed to diversity. As we wake up to our biases, we will want people around us who are dedicated to learning about stereotyping. It's difficult to avoid the topic and yet, people do. Being surrounded by people who are not "tone deaf" to this global conversation is critical. I have removed myself from some friendships where the other person discriminated based on race, gender, weight, and social status, and was not open to a discussion. I didn't blame or shame them, I invited them into a frank discussion, and they decided not to join in. They went so far as to being closed off about any science or data. One of these individuals is a founder of a startup. I am mentoring his only female employee who frequently is excluded.

All these action steps take time, energy, and effort. You may growl about this, saying, *"I'm already too busy."* It's important to say that minor activities add up to significant consequences if they are repeated by and happen to many people. This works both ways. Small unconscious biases can adversely affect us all. Small interferences of bias by many people can benefit us all. We can no longer abdicate responsibility for the inequality in the world. We all must join the conversation and act individually and collectively. While stereotypes were once useful for survival, and still are for ordinary living, this is our opportunity to evolve. "The persistence of such negative reactions may once have had survival value, this is yet another instance of a hardwired response that has lost its relevance. In the modern world, where friendships, collaborations, businesses, and entire economies span the globe in a highly-networked web of interdependence, the ability to create alliances that bypass boundaries of race, nationality, and culture can have bearing on our well-being, our prosperity, our productivity, and perhaps even our survival."[4]

CREDIT ————————————————

1 https://www.merriam-webster.com/dictionary/stereotype

2 Steele, Claude M. (2010). Whistling Vivaldi; How Stereotypes Affect Us and What We Can Do. New York, NY. W. W Norton & Company, Inc. (p. 59-60)

3 Ronson, John. (2015). So, You've Been Publicly Shamed. New York, NY. Riverhead Books. (p 280-281)

4 Banaji, Mahzarin R & Greenwald, Anthony, G. (2013). Blindspot: Hidden Biases of Good People. New York, NY. Random House. (p. 135)

PART THREE

Do You Have Your Back?

CHAPTER 27

WE ARE NOT IMPOSTERS

The paramount relationship we must cultivate is the one with our own self which deeply involves the practice of good self-esteem. Yes, it is a *practice!* How we relate to ourselves directly impacts how we relate to others. Inevitably, in my coaching sessions, in my workshops, and when conversing with friends, the topic of self-love arises. Many terms that have morphed over the years: self-esteem, self-concept, self-love, and the latest buzz term, Imposter Syndrome. All point directly to the way we treat ourselves. Simply put, are we there for ourselves? Do we have our own back? For if we do not, we cannot lead and support others.

Loving others starts with loving ourselves. When we have a healthy level of self-esteem, we can move about the world with compassion because we do not put ourselves on trial by focusing on, exaggerating, or over-identifying with negative aspects of ourselves or our lives. If we continue to conduct our lives in a mental fog, we will suffer. Instead, if we are in support of ourselves, it's not a mystery, we will continue to learn, grow, and evolve. There is zero transformational value in criticizing. Instead, we can cultivate a very rich personal relationship. To do so, we must dedicate effort and energy. Just like the other skills we've discussed, self-esteem is a practice. How we relate to ourselves takes skill and mastery.

The following are some practices to consider in learning how to cultivate self-esteem. They are very useful. I try to embody these and all the practices in this book. At the end of each one, I have added an inquiry with which to experiment.

Commit to live consciously. To have high self-esteem, what is required is to *not* be a stranger or a mystery to *you*. How can we love someone if we don't know them? We can't know ourselves unless we are aware of ourself. All of the practices in Part One speak to being a conscious human being. To live consciously is to be aware of all our actions and that which bears on our existence. When we are committed to living consciously, we are always seeking to expand awareness—a commitment to learning—therefore a commitment to growth as a way of life. When we commit to living consciously, we make a stand for truth.

When we are present, we are moving in concert with what wants to happen, and we respond to life peacefully and in alignment with who we are. If we fail to do this, we are dissociated from our experience and feel dissatisfied. These experiences begin to accumulate and will cause us to become increasingly disjointed. That is when our self-esteem inevitably takes a hit. Think about it. When we engage ourselves and others unconsciously in a way that is not in alignment with who we are, we don't feel good about ourselves. Instead of allowing the self-criticism to hijack us, we can step into the next practice.

Inquiry: How can I live more consciously?

Practice unconditional self-love and self-acceptance. When I talk about the practice of unconditional self-love and self-acceptance, *I do not* mean that you sugarcoat all your activities and behaviors with some superficial affirmations. What is important is that you love and accept yourself—unconditionally—*no matter what.* You may not like, endorse, and condone everything you do. You make mistakes. You harm others. You screw up. Through all these situations, you must have your back! For when you love and accept yourself, then you can hold yourself accountable, learn from any experience, and make changes going forward. You cannot learn and grow from a mistake you do not accept you've made.

Inquiry: Where have I not accepted and loved myself unconditionally, and how can I love and accept all parts of me?

Take responsibility for our actions and life. A powerful way to increase self-esteem is to take ownership for what we've done, take responsibility for our life. Realize that no one is coming to save you. Take an active orientation to life which includes independent thinking rather than passive conformity to others. Taking responsibility is the deep knowing that we oversee our lives, the creator of our activities, the instigator of our well-being, and the conductor leading us to the attainment of our goals. No one else is responsible for our life. We are directly accountable for our actions regardless of our intentions. When we take responsibility, we can recognize when we need help and ask for the support of others without being rescued.

Inquiry: In what parts of my life am I abdicating responsibility, and how can I take responsibility for all aspects of my life?

Assert our authentic self. If we do not assert our authentic selves, we will feel like an imposter. When we fake the reality of who we are, when we disown any part of our experience to avoid others' disapproval, we betray ourselves in the deepest manner. We must be authentic in our dealings with ourselves and others so that we elicit self-respect. With the willingness to stand up for ourselves and our ideas in appropriate ways, in appropriate circumstances, we invite others to stand up for their own. By asserting ourselves, we confront the challenges of life by expanding the boundaries of our willingness to cope. Therefore, we raise our personal power. We build self-trust when we lunge ourselves further into the universe and assert our existence.

Inquiry: How can I assert myself more authentically and know that I have a right to exist?

Build our self-efficacy. Simply with self-efficacy, we can function in life by setting goals, evaluating your progress, adjusting when necessary, so that we meet our goals. We are productive. Productivity is *very* important; however, understand that the outcome to strive for here is not to prove ourselves or to avoid the fear of failure. Our aim instead is self-expression rather than self-justification. When we are efficacious, we know that achievements do not prove our worth and the process of achieving is how we develop our competence at living.

Inquiry: How can my productivity act as an expression of who I am?

Be impeccable in our integrity. When we are in high integrity, we will experience high self-esteem. When we are impeccable in our integrity, we show remarkable congruence between what we know, what we profess, and what we do. We tell the truth. We honor our agreements. We deal with others fairly and benevolently. We hold ourselves accountable to support our moral aspirations. We exemplify through our actions our values. When we betray our values, our self-esteem takes a hit. If we are consistent in our integrity, when we experience dishonesty, it will be disturbing to us, and we will feel called to resolve the dissonance and restore our inner sense of moral cleanliness.

Inquiry: In what areas of my life am I out of integrity, and what action can I take to come back into integrity?

Actively develop our skill for kindness and compassion. Research suggests that high self-compassion and kindness increases well-being. Kindness and compassion begin with how we treat ourselves. We can build a frame of mind for compassion by putting our attention on self-kindness instead of self-judgment. We can create a sense of common humanity instead of isolation. We can expand into stillness instead of identification when confronting negative self-relevant thoughts and emotions. All this requires of us is a commitment to be caring and understanding with ourselves rather than being harshly critical or judgmental. We are all are imperfect, we fail and make mistakes. Our flawed condition is connected to the shared human condition; we will cultivate compassion.

Inquiry: How can I increase my kindness and compassion moment-to-moment?

See ourselves. In the absence of conscious awareness for our self-esteem, we unconsciously adopt opinions of ourselves that we inherited from our familial, social, and cultural backgrounds. To build self-esteem in children, we must lea to *see* them. Parents do the best they can or can't, and unfortunately, many of us weren't psychologically seen as a child. Many people experienced severe trauma during their childhood. These experiences are a blow to childhood development and, ultimately, self-esteem. We can't go back and erase the past; however, we *can* begin to see ourselves fully and be there for ourselves. All that is required is for us to give ourselves permission to see ourselves and, in turn, be seen by others.

Inquiry: What parts of me do I hide from and am not willing to see, and how can I see them, embrace them, and love them?

Each of these practices can stand alone. However, we must become skillful at all of them to build a core foundation of self-esteem. Consider the impact of low self-esteem. These are real-life examples:

- The leader who deflects positive feedback because he is so self-critical, he is only willing to pay attention to negative feedback, to "what he does wrong."

- The data scientist researcher who is never "good enough" in her eyes. She is not able to speak up at meetings to express her point of view.

- The senior executive who allowed his self-confidence to tumble when he made a mistake. Rather than learning through the experience, he categorized himself as "I am bad."

- The software engineer who only shares what's going well for him and avoids talking about when he struggles for fear of criticism.

- The C-Suite executive who looks all put together on the inside but is experiencing body pain and anxiety attacks on the inside. She is so dissociated with her experience of herself, no one really knows her.

- Some of the people I come across have talent and experience, even with strong self-efficacy, but consider themselves frauds, and imposters because they can't internalize their accomplishments.

- The team that is committed to drama and lack of healthy responsibility creates a culture of no accountability—a blow to everyone's self-esteem.

Consider the impact of high self-esteem with these real-life examples:

- The successful executive, who, after letting her emotions pass, blurted, "I just want to be me," an insight in favor of her self-esteem

- The C-Suite executive who creates a culture of learning, enabling the company to adapt in an information age

- The lawyer who is committed to the practices above and is flourishing in a very unconscious environment

- The software engineer who is kind and compassionate but can exercise healthy boundaries when treated poorly

- The magazine editor who can celebrate the wins of his colleagues regardless of what's going on his life

- The managing director who is easily able to lead more qualified people without feeling intimidated

- The founder, whose company failed and went out of business, who asked simply, "How can I feel my feelings and learn from this experience?"

Clean Up Your Messes. It's time to shift the good versus bad and right versus wrong paradigms. Falling into, *"This is good,"* or *"This is bad,"* *"This is right,"* or *"This is wrong,"* is a strong trap and an invitation for low self-esteem. As we experience moral efficacy, we become a master of the above practices.

When we start to categorize everything as good or bad, right or wrong, we suffer. We are always evaluating ourselves under this paradigm. A life of self-evaluation is exhausting. There are consequences to all of our actions, so merely ask, *"Where are my actions harmful, and how can I take responsibility?"*

We need strength of mind and character to not act out harmfully. We get triggered, we act out, we harm others—this is inevitable. We interpret these actions as personal by subscribing to self-deprecating thoughts. When we do harm others, and we will, simply take responsibility, and repair any consequences to the actions. Then learn and evolve from the experience. Simply, *clean up our messes.* For when we clean up any harm we've done, we have our back and are standing up for ourselves in the face of a challenge. Our self-esteem grows. *"How can I . . .?"* versus *"Why do I . . .?* If you notice the inquiry questions above, they begin with, *"How can I . . .?"* This is by design. When we start with, *"Why do I . . .?"* questions, we invite self-criticism. It is useful to debrief our actions for learning. But by beginning with, *"Why do I . . .?"* our minds usually grab onto this, and internal drama begins. This is unproductive. When we begin with, *"How can I . . .?"* we are inviting forward action toward self-esteem and evolution. Simply, *why* takes us into criticizing the past and *how* escorts us into the present, and how we want to be going forward.

Take an inventory of self-esteem. It is my experience that this is how people get in their way and hold themselves back. I am repeating it and will *keep* repeating it: consciousness is a practice and self-esteem is at the top of the list of importance. We can become masterful at relating to ourselves, and see what happens in all of our other relationships. To take inventory, go to www.abigailstason.com and download the two-page document called *Self-Concept.* Take note of what you are or aren't implementing, and look for opportunities to increase your self-esteem. Don't be intimidated if it all seems new to you. That just means you have more room to learn. Send me a note. I'd love to hear from you.

PART FOUR

Go Deeper—Go Direct

CHAPTER 28

WAKE UP TO OUR TRUE NATURE— THE TRUTH OF WHO WE ARE

Inevitably, what we are all seeking is peace, freedom, and love. The significant betrayal is we tell ourselves we *must* do something to be peaceful, to be free, to receive love. The truth of who we are *is* peace, freedom, and love. Our true nature is pure *being-ness* and consciousness.

Experiences, thoughts, friends, relationships, jobs, our bodies, the weather, all come and go as phenomena. We are that which *does not come and go*, that which *is always here*—pure awareness and consciousness. At any time, we can directly open to what's always here. When we identify with what comes and goes, we suffer.

We Are Not Our Bodies

When we identify with our bodies, we suffer. Our body comes and goes. When we can view them as an impersonal nervous system, we can attend to them just as we would a garden. If we tend the garden, it will flourish. If we ignore the garden, it will become overgrown with weeds, become messy, even die in harsh conditions. There are no guarantees except that one day the body will cease to exist.

Our nervous systems are incredibly vulnerable, and we are a world of doers. We ignore the signals from our bodies and overload our nervous system with experiences. If our car is overheating, would we keep driving, or would we pull over? We would pull over and evaluate what's happening, of course. With our bodies, however, we keep driving, overheating our nervous systems.

It's not personal, and it's all personal. We suffer by taking things personally. As I mentioned in another chapter, the human body is an organism. The organism's *primary* function and sole purpose is to survive. Our nervous system is scanning the environment for what's wrong, in anticipation of danger. Therefore, when my body is scanning yours for friend or foe, it assumes foe. *It is not personal.* The body wants to survive, and this is helpful! And *it is entirely personal.* Science proves everything my organism does and affects other organisms. Furthermore, recent studies show that the brain distinguishes no difference between physical, emotional, and social pain. If you verbally attack me, I experience your attack the same as if you broke my arm. Here we are being asked to evolve. In this information age, we are no longer working with our bodies, picking cotton, and operating heavy machinery. Everything is being automated. Roles are shifting to sharing knowledge, and information is a most valued skill. What we are left with is an opportunity to shift to interacting with others more consciously. We must know when the organism is in survival mode, and be aware of the impact of our actions on others.

Take responsibility when you cause harm. The organism is a series of energetic biochemical events and, left to its own devices, will react in ways that are inappropriate. How we were raised, our genes, our environment, and a host of other factors determine how the biochemical reaction responds to experiences, other organisms, and to life. We get triggered, we act out, we harm others; this is inevitable, *and* we interpret these actions as very personal attacks by labeling ourselves or others as the enemy. Others act out and start judging the people who harmed them—the battle starts. We suffer in conflict with others.

It's not personal. This is *not* an oversimplification. When we *do* harm to others, and we will, we must simply take responsibility, and repair any consequences to the action. Then we learn and evolve from the experience. *Clean up the mess.* This is where we can support each other and where we need each other. Because the nervous system event can be so strong, we may not realize we are triggered. We may not be able to be connected to our experience so that we can hold ourselves accountable. If we are surrounded with people who help us see when we caused harm, we can repair any damage. And when we see someone harming another, we can point it out non-judgmentally.

What's very easy to distinguish is harmful physical behavior. When we physically harm someone, the damage is seen immediately and distinctly. Let's be clear, any flavor or blaming, shaming, or criticizing is *equally as harmful.* Yelling obscenities at someone can be even more harmful. It's time we start to recognize that the verbal punches we throw at each other do serious damage to us individually and collectively. Everyone's self-esteem is diminished when we don't clean up our messes. Part Three explains how to get rid of the good versus the bad and the right versus the wrong paradigm. Instead, ask, "Did I cause harm?" If so, make amends. It's that simple.

Emotions are survival energy. We suffer by surviving instead of grabbing the opportunity to evolve. Part One describes a framework on how to capture the wisdom in emotions. This can be very useful. To come closer and more direct to the truth of who we are, we realize that emotions are just waves of energy that support the nervous system to survive. The basis of each emotion is fear. When we realize this, we are free to let emotional energy flow. We are not born to hate. We are born to survive. Remember the organism's sole purpose is to survive.

- **Anger**—what to resist to survive
- **Sadness**—you have lost something in which you invested energy, something crucial for your survival

- **Joy**—evolutionary signal we are doing something right for survival

- **Fear**—what to avoid for survival and a warning to the tribe

- **Sexual**—propagate so that your genes are passed on, and the species survives

- **Disgust**—concrete behavior to get rid of something toxic, spit it out to survive

- **Love**—affection developed so that the tribe sticks together, strength in numbers

Instead of suppressing or repressing our emotional energy, we can evolve past survival mode by simply letting this energy flow through our nervous systems by breathing and providing our bodies with what they need for this biochemical event to continue as easily and efficiently as possible.

Pain and pleasure versus suffering. It becomes very challenging to not identify with the body during times of great pain or great pleasure. To say that pain and pleasure are two common experiences of the body is stating the obvious. When we add to these experiences, we suffer.

Early in 2017, I herniated a disc in my back and was struck with very severe sciatic pain. I chose to have surgery. The pain was as excruciating as my recovery. It was a traumatic experience for my nervous system. We suffer when we add to the pain by fighting it, trying to make it go away, and attempting to distract ourselves from the experience of feeling victimized. I can remember being pulled into all these strategies. Instead of adding to my pain, I would simply breathe through the waves, making myself as comfortable as possible, using some painkillers, and reaching out for emotional, mental, and physical support. I acted in any direction that was most in favor of supporting my nervous system through this experience.

Yes, this is easier said than done, and I feel so much compassion for people who have chronic pain and fatal diseases. Pain is exhausting. When we add to it, however, we make it worse; hence the unnecessary suffering added to an already overwhelming experience.

We can suffer from pleasure, too. Instead of just allowing it to exist and experience the good feelings, letting this energy pass, we start to want to *keep* it. We wonder if we will ever feel this way again. We want *more* because we don't *want it to end.* Pleasurable experiences are already enough for our nervous systems, but when we add to them, we suffer. The nervous system mostly seeks homeostasis and will naturally be impacted by intense painful or pleasurable experiences.

Become a master of understanding the nervous system. These are just some of the things that impact the "cocktail" experience of the nervous system: endocrinology, proteins, neuroscience, cardiovascular, genetics, environment, trauma, personality, temperament, childhood experiences, illness, culture, and societal norms. They come together to form a response in our interactions. Should we become therapists or doctors to understand all of this? Not at all. But we do need to understand on a fundamental level that the body is *biology* and not who *we are.* Just as we learn to drive and take care of a car, we can increase our level of awareness and engagement in understanding the body. We can't possibly understand all the inner workings of our nervous systems, but we can recognize this, choose to keep an eye on our activities *and* make supporting our nervous system a priority.

The body reflects being-ness. The body will come and go. While we are not our nervous system, the body is a manifestation of being-ness. When we open to what's always here, we will realize that life force energy flowing through the body is beyond our control because we *are* that life force energy—*pure being-ness*—not the skin and bones that make up the body.

We Are Not Our Thoughts

When we identify with our thoughts, we suffer in countless ways. Thoughts come and go, and when we focus on what comes and goes, we are not satisfied. Life is a series of waves of energy pulsing. The question to ask is, 'Where do I put my allegiance?" Do we put it on what comes and goes (our thoughts) or on what is always here? When we can view our thoughts phenomena, then we can let them pass by like a breeze. Instead, we identify with them, treat them as real, and then suffer in the internal mental wrestling match of our minds. We align our activities to what comes and goes which is an exercise in futility. We listen to mental chatter instead of being in our direct experience.

We suffer in the stream of thoughts of worry. Worrying is a national pastime. When we worry, we suffer. We worry about *everything*. In creating this mind swirl, we move farther and farther from the truth and our direct experience.

We worry about the past or the future. We worry about a meeting we are attending. We worry that it will rain. We worry about the profitability of our business. We worry about that promotion and whether we are qualified. We worry that we are worrying too much and can't sleep. Our thoughts spin out of control, instead of stopping to investigate and asking, "Is any of this true?" See if these sound familiar.

- What if I don't get that promotion?
- What if they don't like me?
- What if I screw it up?
- What if I never find a life partner?
- What if it rains?
- What will happen if/when . . ?
- I'm a fraud, and what if they find out?

By all means, don't adopt a "don't worry, be happy" disposition. What *is* useful is to pay attention to anything for which we should genuinely be concerned. Concern is different than worry. Worry is the spin of thoughts. Concern is a more organic energy. There *may* be some aspect of the experience to be *concerned* about that will guide us in aligned, intelligent action. Be concerned about that.

One day I was in my car on the way to meet someone for coffee. I was thinking about a keynote speech I was to deliver in two weeks. The worry began. I had the thought, *What if I screw it up?* Here I am, in my car, driving, with nothing else to do but to get to a coffee shop where I was meeting someone to discuss bringing my program (all the skills in this book) into their company.

The thought, *What if I screw it up?* invited me down the rabbit hole of suffering. In the past, I would grab onto the thought, treat it as reality, and add to it with inner dialog such as, *If I screw it up, no one will hire me. They won't listen to the points I'm making. I won't make an impact. No one will like me. That will be bad, very bad. I am bad.* Now, imagine if I identified with these thoughts, especially the last one —*I am bad.* By treating this thought as reality, I suffered, and I affected my ability to give an effective speech.

Now I investigate such thoughts. Therefore, in the moment, I noticed myself headed down the rabbit hole. I stop and ask myself, *Is there anything to be concerned with right now regarding my speech?* Because it is *smart* to pay attention to concern energy. The speech I was to give was to a large crowd, about a thousand people. I wanted to perform in alignment with my experience and be prepared. A thousand people were taking time out of their day to hear what I had to say. I needed to be sure I was on top of my game. (I am still driving to the coffee shop.) My intelligent concern is, *I do feel concerned that I won't be clear during my speech, so I want to make sure I am prepared. Right now, I am about to meet someone for coffee, and, when I get home later, I want to run through my notes again.*

Worry is *distraction*. Concern is *energy* to which we need to pay attention.

We suffer in the stream of thoughts of purpose. Thoughts such as, *What is my purpose? I have to live out my purpose! I'm not in my purpose*, invite self-doubt and diminished self-esteem, leading to suffering. It's important to distinguish between purpose and role.

Our purpose is to wake up and love each other, and as a human species, we are being asked to evolve.

With that context, ask what role do we want play? We play varied roles in our lives: executive, doctor, parent, friend, engineer, etc. Investigate this. When we let go of the overloaded term *purpose*, we are equipped to have a more intelligent conversation about our role on this planet, how we want to contribute, how we want to spend our time.

Roles are changing and forever vulnerable as we continue and to evolve and grow in society.

- Gender roles are changing. No longer is the "man of the house" the main breadwinner, and no longer is it expected that women stay home. Similarly, men can tune into what they most want rather than being forced by society to provide for a family.

- Coal miners' roles are changing. Coal is becoming outdated and even for those mines where workers exist, their jobs have been automated and continue to be automated. This is true of many fossil fuel industries.

- Trucking industry roles are changing as self-driving trucks have been invented. These individuals now must learn computer skills to remotely "drive" trucks when they exit the highway.

- Advertising roles are being affected as the way the world uses ads is being reinvented. Social media is evolving exponentially as a means of marketing and advertising.

- Stock traders are being replaced by technology engineers so computers can more accurately perform calculations that formerly took people countless hours.

- Individuals in the medical field are affected by technology and must keep up with advancements. New jobs are emerging every day as new equipment and methods of treatment are developed.

- Artificial intelligence is in its infancy so we cannot predict its impact, but we can surmise it will be significant on the roles we play in the world.

- The role of parent changes in a lifetime. At first, offspring are dependent upon their parents, but as children grow up, the dynamic of parent-to-child changes to adult-to-adult.

Every industry is being affected by advances in technology and a lifelong commitment to learning is imperative. The skills required to do our jobs is forever changing, so ongoing technical learning is critical. This is obvious and yet we don't set up our lives with the agility to adapt, so our instinctual survival mode is activated. Furthermore, by identifying with a role, we suffer. Imagine being a stock trader and learning my role is being replaced by a computer engineer. If we identify with our role as who we are, what happens if the job goes away? Are we worthless? Of course not! But it will be necessary to find another job. If we have identified with being a stock trader and locked into this without awakening to the fact that roles are changing, we will be devastated when the role is eliminated and we will go into survival or drama mode.

With a background on Wall Street, I witnessed this in the crash of 2008. I worked at Merrill Lynch, and the morning Merrill was bought by Bank of America, instead of being grateful that the company was still in existence, and they still had jobs, people went into survival mode. I overheard actual discussions of the question, "Who are we if we are not Merrill Lynch employees?"

People started back-stabbing, fighting for positions—it was as if they were fighting for their lives. When I left the industry, people were shocked that I "had the courage to leave" after nineteen years. Many people said, "How can you leave? This is your life!" I can remember thinking, *Wall Street executive is not who I am. This is my role, and it's time for my role to change. Where there is consistency in my role is with regard to leadership. I am always leading something. My role now is to help develop humans who are awake and conscious leaders.*

Don't oversimplify or diminish the importance of choosing roles. They are necessary and are how we function in societies. Employment roles are how we earn money and provide for ourselves. Those of mother, father, mentor, elected official, etc. are how we collaborate in the world and communicate. It is when we identify with a role that *comes and goes* that we will never be satisfied, and we suffer.

As soon as I review *role* versus *purpose* with my clients, participants in my workshops, and my friends, it's as if a light goes off within them, and they immediately relax. When we start to entangle roles with purpose, we provide fodder for the mind to complicate matters on something that is quite simple.

We suffer in the stream of thoughts of complexity. Life is complex enough, and we don't need to add to it. We have many challenges and hurdles. The direct experience of these adds fresh and organic complexity where complexity is due. We don't need to add to it by making it hard. Life can also be simple when simple is due. There's no need to oversimplify or complicate matters. Let them be—as they are.

We suffer in the stream of thoughts of self-doubt. There is zero transformational value in self-criticizing. If we identify with thoughts such as, *I am not good enough, I am not worthy,* or *I am an imposter,* we will be miserable on multiple levels. There is no greater betrayal than when we turn our back on ourselves. Self-esteem, when used for building integrity with our self-concept, is a skill that we can master. Read the chapter on self-esteem again and download the one-page document from the website.

We suffer in the stream of thoughts of *I can be happy when . . .* We are never satisfied and always wanting more. More money, more experiences, a better job, the perfect spouse, a bigger house. We are a materialistic society, and we use materialism as the measure of our success and fulfillment. When we consider who we are based on our accumulation of anything, we suffer, *even* philanthropically. "If I give enough to those less fortunate, then I will be happy." No amount of experiences, wealth, etc., will match the satisfaction of knowing the truth of who we are. Life is challenging, and if we are expecting to be happy all the time, we are operating in an illusion. It is a dichotomy, but *striving to be happy* is a recipe for disaster.

We suffer in the stream of thoughts of emotions. We lock onto our emotions as who we are instead of treating them as life force energy forever pulsing through the body. We repress feelings and move into a stream of thoughts and treat that as our experience. Emotions are an experience of the body, not the truth of who we are. If we identify with, *I am an angry person*, imagine the implications. Anger comes and goes; it's a short psychosomatic experience of the body. If we walk around incorporating the thought, *I am an angry person*, we are blocking truth and reality. We are in a thought and have betrayed the truth of our bodily experience, as well as the truth of who we are. What is truer is, *There is a wave of energy passing through my nervous system right now.*

We are addicted to our thoughts. We may not be able to recognize conditioning and only know life as our thoughts. This becomes an addiction because, by identifying with our thoughts, it soothes our discomfort with the inconvenience of truth. A lazy mind makes for lazy action. It takes strength of mind and character to tell the truth, to speak the relative truth of our experience, and to speak the absolute truth that we are not separate. Don't wonder if *I am not this body, and I am not my thoughts, who am I?* Stop and explore this thoroughly.

CHAPTER 29

STOPPING IS THE ULTIMATE DISRUPTER

Even stop the stopping.

—GANGAJI

I can remember sitting in satsang with my teacher when she said, "You already know how to go, so stop. Stop everything." It was as if a bolt of lightning hit me. The fresh insight came. *That's heresy!* and *I'm in!* I realized that *stopping* is the ultimate disrupter.

It's time to make this word *stop* an essential part of our vocabulary. Stopping is the one of the most uncomfortable experiences for anyone. We are a world of doers. We fill our time with tasks, information, social media, experiences, thoughts—anything to avoid being still. We are conditioned to go, go, go, and to go faster. The pressure we put on ourselves to engage in activities is unreasonable and unrealistic. Our nervous systems can only handle so much activity. As my teacher said, "We are experts at going. It's time to become experts at stopping." This is an invitation to stop. Stop everything. Even stop the stopping because as doers, we will even make stopping a *doing*.

We ignore the signals of burnout and are in crisis mode. We betray the truth of who we are by placing our interest in what comes and goes. This is *conditioning*. To overcome conditioning, we need strength of mind and strength of character. Conditioning is useful in certain circumstances, but left uninvestigated, we are not able to discover the truth as it emerges. This means letting go of control and letting go of what we think will happen. Stopping allows us to disrupt conditioning and open to what's always here—to experience life directly—as it unfolds. *not* as we think it should be.

We can stop, investigate, and tell the truth. When we stop and are still, we can open to our direct experience. This is what I refer to as *being* versus doing. When we are in our direct experience, we will be freshly and organically informed by pure intelligence and wisdom from which aligned action or non-action appears. From stillness, our response will be appropriate.

A simple analogy is this: we are spending the day at a pool, relaxing on the lounges, and begin to talk about getting in the water.

Abby: "I don't know if I want to swim today."

Client: "I may dive right in."

Abby: "I may do a cannonball."

Client: "Do you think the water is warm or cold?"

Abby: "I don't know. I'll bet it's cold."

Client: "What if we make a splash and get everyone wet?"

Abby: "We would be in trouble then."

Client: "It's not the worst. I've been in trouble before, not fun."

Abby: "Last time we swam together, all you wanted to do was race."

Client: "You were cranky that day."

Abby: "I still don't know if I want to swim today. But this is the last chance I'll have. What a bummer summer is ending."

This stream of thoughts can go on and on. I use this innocuous example because this is what we do. We talk about our experience or *think* about them rather than *being in them*—this is the addiction. To apply *stop* here, simply stop talking. Be still. Investigate and tell the truth. By stopping and investigating, the truth will come out and we will recognize we are swirling in *thoughts* about the pool. When we recognize this, we can be still to see what wants to happen as it emerges. We cannot know what will happen, but we can trust that we will be guided by deeper wisdom rather than a stream of thoughts.

Again, the swimming pool scenario is innocuous. Now apply this to a challenge you've faced. When I left Wall Street to become a consciousness facilitator, I started over. It was a new beginning. When I caught myself in my thoughts, I stopped and asked, *What's here? What wants to happen next?* From that place, I planned and strategized rather than assuming I knew what was to happen. Because any time we think we know what will happen, we shut down curiosity and the mystery of possibilities. *There is no formula for life.*

The Antitheses of Woo-Hoo

The practical application of what has been discussed here is enormous. Again, check it out for yourself. Stop and investigate. Tell the truth. This is no small matter and requires maturity. There is a certain level of reflection that is required for human beings. The relative truth is very inconvenient and can be extremely disruptive. By telling the relative truth, we are required to take responsibility for our actions and for peace.

What does this have to do with leadership? Everything! Part One through Four provide skills to develop *you*. These are extremely useful and will show you ways to navigate the day-to-day. The goal is to direct you *at any time* to the absolute truth of who you are. When we turn away from the truth of who we are, we suffer and cannot effectively lead. There is nowhere to go, nothing to do but open ourselves to experience directly what is always here. When we experience life directly, *true life force energy,* we have access to pure intelligence and wisdom. We do not respond from fear. We make our primary marriage to truth, and in doing so, are free, peaceful, and loving.

If you find yourself hungering for life, *stop and be still.* Check it out. You will find *you are life.*

PART FIVE

Join the Revolution

CHAPTER 30

ANSWER THE WAKE-UP CALL TO HUMANITY

Humanity has evolved throughout the ages, and it's time now to be in the driver's seat for our species. To evolve consciously is to be aware of how we are growing and developing—to be awake to how our evolution impacts humanity and the world around us. We can let go of the evolutionary patterns that are no longer of service. We must choose to intentionally to move away from an instinctual survival mode, to move away from cultural and societal norms that are not in favor of everyone. Globalization is forcing us to evolve.

You can realize the interconnectedness of us all, and transform business through that connection, through relationship. The most significant impact we can make in the world is the moment-to-moment choice to be awake to our actions, to be conscious and to choose love and compassion. Switching from unconscious to conscious activities requires commitment, energy, and courage to stand alone in the face of those choosing to stay asleep. The payoff is huge in the form of growth, learning, and vitality.

There are a variety of choices we make every day that can impact our individual and collective worlds—conscious choices for sustainable impact in the world. When we are proactive and conscious in our choices, we create a ripple effect and evolve consciously as if with a compass.

We have been sailing without a compass for too long, and we are see the effects through global crises. Here are a few thoughts on how consciousness can be our guide across all facets of life so that we can make a difference in the world.

Be a conscious and evolved human being. Awakening starts with us. When we are awake, we invite others to wake up. The possibilities of discovery are endless. It's time for us to come together with love and compassion—consciously. We cannot be in a mental fog and relate to ourselves. Consciousness is not asking for perfection. Instead, it's asking for awareness, which bears on all of our thoughts, actions, and beliefs, as well as how we affect the world around us. When we are aware of ourselves, we can be mindful of others we relate to. And when we relate with others, conditioning and unconscious commitments invite autopilot and survival. Whether work or personal, when we are not conscious in relationship, drama, and inauthentic connection will ensue. This is especially true of our relationships with our intimate partners and close work colleagues. Consciously designing the relationship, we want leads to accelerated growth, discovery, and peace. All the practices in this book will empower us to create conscious, loving relationships.

High performing conscious teams. When we are conscious human beings, we contribute to an evolved team. High-performing conscious teams are agile and can adapt in this information age. Not distracted by surviving, drama, and conflict, conscious teams know how to channel life force energy productively. These teams know that the primary focus is being connected to each other, for without connection, projects do not move forward and innovation is halted.

Create a conscious culture. We must be the culture we want to create and step out of victim mode and into empowerment by asking, "How do I contribute to the culture that is around me?" We can consciously create the culture that is good of all of us. We *are* the culture, creating it with each moment of choice—to be conscious or not, to be loving or not, to be compassionate or not. Now is the time to consciously choose how to treat ourselves and others. Let this book serve as your culture manual.

Awakened societies in favor of humanity and the planet. We can create a world of conscious individuals, and it begins with *us*. Now is the time to choose to be a creator in the world versus a consumer, choosing for the benefit of all, paying attention consciously to what and how we consume food, goods, planetary resources, media, and electronics. Small steps toward sustainability each day can impact our planet. We can be skillful stewards of the planet's resources through every choice we make. By making sustainable choices in favor of the good of all, over time, can swing the pendulum the other way toward a more connected way of being. We can change the world along the way.

Not for the faint of heart. I want to leave you with this repeated acknowledgment. What I am suggesting here is simply said but not so simply done. I am not an idealist with some pie in the sky rhetoric. Waking up is not for the faint of heart. This is not a casual invitation. What is required of us all is energy, attention, and investigation. Globalization presents very complex and heartbreaking challenges. The invitation is to rise to these challenges to become a part of the transition team for a global awakening. If you are reading this book, you are up for the challenge. The alarm is ringing—join me in answering the wake-up call.

CHAPTER 31

NEXT STEPS—THERE IS ALWAYS MORE

Start practicing. *Yes,* when we start using these skills in our day-to-day we will grow and evolve. Our choices in each moment in favor of conscious evolution are the most impactful and relevant actions we can take. We to choose consciousness moment, after moment, after moment. Remember, it is not about *perfection*; it is about *awareness.*

Enlist an evolution partner. Business brings us together. Use this forum to experiment with others. It will accelerate your growth and development when learning alongside others.

Download resources. Go to www.abigailstason.com for worksheets and additional resources. For your convenience, there are two bonus chapters.

- **Improv as a Path to Presence**
- **Conscious Appreciation—Leading with Positive Energy**

Bring Conscious Leadership to Your Organization.

- 1:1 Executive Facilitation
- Organizational Design
- Team Workshops
- Silent Retreats

Spread the word. Tell others about the skills in this book, so those who are less fortunate have access to skills that will directly impact their lives.

Connect. I would love to hear from you and what you are learning on your evolutionary journey:

www.abigailstason.com

abby@abigailstason.com

(415) 847-1536

Give back. Gift this book to someone you care about, and if you have benefited from *Evolution Revolution,* please acknowledge the global awakening by contributing to the Gangaji Foundation. I am a monthly donor and volunteer.

www.gangaji.org

RESOURCES

I f it is spiritual awakening you are craving, I recommend you read anything by my spiritual teacher Gangaji. I have come across many teach-
ers and Gangaji is the "real deal." She shares a simple message: "This
is an invitation to shift your allegiance from the activities of your mind
to the eternal presence of your being." Gangaji has walked the path of
the lineage of Sri Ramana Maharishi and Sri H.W.L. Poonja "Papaji."

We live in a time when there is so much valuable *new* research,
neuroscience, and information available. There are also some theories
that have been around for years which we are finally beginning to understand and incorporate. You can read about them in some of my favorite
books.

- Banaji, Mahzarin R. & Greenwald, Anthony, G. (2013). *Blindspot: Hidden Biases of Good People.* New York, NY. Random House.

- Branden, Nathaniel. (1994). *The Six Pillars of Self-Esteem.* New York, NY. Bantam.

- Branden, Nathaniel. (1971). *The Disowned Self: An Illuminating Analysis of One of the Most Important Problems of Our Time: Self-Alienation.* Los Angeles, CA. Bantam.

- Branden, Nathaniel. (1997). *The Art of Living Consciously: The Power of Awareness to Transform Everyday Life.* New York, NY. Fireside.

- Csikszentmihalyi, Mihaly. (1990). *Flow: The Psychology of Optimal Experience:* New York, NY. First Harper.

- Dweck Ph.D., Carol. (2006). *Mindset: The New Psychology of Success: How We Can Learn to Fulfill Our Potential.* New York, NY. Ballantine.

- Duhigg, Charles. (2012). *The Power of Habit: Why We Do What We Do in Life and Business.* New York, NY. Random House.

- Hayden, Gina. (2006). *Becoming A Conscious Leader: How to Lead Successfully in A World That's Waking Up.* UK. Panacea Books.

- Hollis Ph.D., James. (2007). *Why Good People Do Bad Things: Understanding Our Darker Selves.* New York, NY. Gotham Books.

- Huffington, Arianna. (2016). *The Sleep Revolution.* New York, NY. Random House.

- Kahneman, Daniel. (2011). *Thinking Fast and Slow.* New York, NY. Farrar, Straus, and Giroux.

- Sapolsky, Robert M. (2017). *Behave: The Biology of Humans at Our Best and Worst.* New York, NY. Penguin Press.

- Sapolsky, Robert M. (2004). *Why Zebras Don't Get Ulcers: The Acclaimed Guide to Stress-Related Diseases, and Coping.* New York, NY. St. Martin's Press.

- Steele, Claude M. (2010). *Whistling Vivaldi: How Stereotypes Affect Us and What We Can Do.* New York, NY. W. W. Norton and Company.

ACKNOWLEDGMENTS

I would like to extend my deep love and gratitude to my teacher, Gangaji. Your presence invites truth, peace, and freedom. Thank you for teaching me to stop and open and to experience what does not come and go. Meeting Gangaji was one of the most powerful experiences of my life. (www.gangaji.org)

I appreciate Gay and Kathlyn Hendricks for providing the opportunity for me to stand for conscious evolution, self-esteem, and my north star.

Thank you to my clients, who continue to ask for "the how" of consciousness in action and encourage me to share my experience in the world. Without their constant thirst for something bigger than themselves and their courage to be on this journey with me, this book would not be here.

Thanks to my friends and loved ones who continued to encourage, champion, and be *for* me in my constant vigilance for truth, awakening, and peace. Thank you for holding me accountable to everything in this book.

With love and gratitude,
Abby

ABOUT ABBY

A former Wall Street executive, Abby has over 40,000 hours of experience leading teams and groups. A visionary with passion for self-esteem, consciousness, and purposeful and creative work environments, Abby has designed and implemented practices to enable her clients to be congruent while meeting the expectations of their organizations.

Abby teaches executives how to be real, highly effective, connected, and evolved individuals and leaders; how to live into their human potential. Abby's style is about converting spiritual concepts into pragmatic practices to support evolution in our day-to-day world. Her approach meets the requirements of the next generations, new paradigms in business, conscious cultures, and expanding consciousness.

Originally from the east coast, she lives in Mill Valley, California and enjoys the outdoors, hiking, riding her boogie board, meandering through Farmers' Markets, and exploring consciousness and transformation with others.

www.abigailstason.com